THE
JAMES SPRUNT STUDIES
IN HISTORY
AND POLITICAL SCIENCE

Published under the Direction of
the Departments of History and Political Science
of The University of North Carolina at Chapel Hill

VOLUME 57

Editors

J. CARLYLE SITTERSON, *Chairman*

FEDERICO G. GIL

JOHN D. MARTZ

GEORGE D. TAYLOR

GEORGE B. TINDALL

SOUTHERN WRITERS AND THE NEW SOUTH MOVEMENT, 1865–1913

by
Wayne Mixon

CHAPEL HILL
THE UNIVERSITY OF NORTH CAROLINA PRESS

© 1980 The University of North Carolina Press
All rights reserved
Manufactured in the United States of America
Cloth edition, ISBN 0-8078-5157-8
Paper edition, ISBN 0-8078-5057-8
Library of Congress Catalog Card Number 79-16606

Library of Congress Cataloging in Publication Data

Mixon, Wayne.
    Southern writers and the New South movement,
1865–1913.

    (The James Sprunt studies in history and
political science; v. 57)
    Bibliography: p.
    Includes index.
    1. American literature—Southern States—History
and criticism. 2. Literature and society—
Southern States. 3. Southern States—History–
1865– 4. Southern States—Civilization. I. Title.
II. Series: James Sprunt studies in history and
political science; v. 57.
PS261.M5   810'.9'975   79-16606
ISBN 0-8078-5057-8
ISBN 0-8078-5058-6 pbk.

To Fran

CONTENTS

ACKNOWLEDGMENTS

Whatever merit this work may have derives largely from the advice and criticism of Professors George Brown Tindall and Louis D. Rubin, Jr., of the University of North Carolina at Chapel Hill, who guided the study from start to finish. With patience and good humor, they shared willingly their knowledge of Southern history and literature, steering me clear of errors in fact, judgment, and style. It was a privilege to work with them.

Professors Peter F. Walker, J. Carlyle Sitterson, Frank W. Ryan, Donald G. Mathews, and Elisha P. Douglass, all of the University of North Carolina, read the manuscript in various stages of preparation and offered pertinent suggestions. Thanks are due, too, to Dr. John G. Barnwell, Mr. George T. Crutchfield, and Dr. Jerry W. Iles, and to Professors William L. Andrews of Texas Tech University, Daniel W. Hollis of the University of South Carolina, Vinton M. Prince, Jr., of Shaw University, William K. Scarborough and John Ray Skates, Jr., of the University of Southern Mississippi–Hattiesburg, B. Howard Welsh of the University of Southern Mississippi–Natchez, and Wilfred C. Platt, Jr., of Mercer University. I should like also to thank the University of North Carolina Press, especially Mr. Malcolm L. Call, editor-in-chief, Mrs. Gwen Duffey, managing editor, and Mrs. Barbara Palmer, copy editor. Any errors that remain in the work are my responsibility alone.

The staffs of the libraries of the University of North Carolina, Duke University, the University of Southern Mississippi (Hattiesburg and Natchez campuses), and Mercer University were helpful, especially in securing materials not readily accessible. Grants by the University of Southern Mississippi and Mercer University helped me complete the manuscript; I am grateful to Dr. Charles W. Moorman of the University of Southern Mississippi and to Dr. R. Kirby Godsey of Mercer University for their assistance in those matters. Miss Bessie Killebrew and Mrs. Diane Wheat skillfully typed the manuscript. The editors of the *Southern Humanities Review* and the *Georgia Historical Quarterly* graciously gave permission to reprint portions of the work published in those journals.

All my family, and particularly my parents, Cornelius Burch and Lucille Daughtry Mixon, know my debt to them. My children, Phillip and Eleanor, bore my absorption in this project better than I had any right to expect. More than anyone else, my wife Fran, who not only endured my long obsession with this endeavor but encouraged me to stick with it, deserves and has my gratitude.

SOUTHERN WRITERS
AND THE
NEW SOUTH MOVEMENT,
1865–1913

INTRODUCTION:
WHITHER THE POSTBELLUM SOUTH?

Even as Union armies were sealing the fate of the Old South in 1865, there were men speaking of a New South. Within a few years, in such unlikely places as Charleston and New Orleans, bastions of the Old Order, and in the newer towns of Atlanta and Birmingham, optimists took hope from defeat, envisioning a society that, if less grand on the surface, would be stronger at the center than the plantation order of the antebellum South. By the 1880s, one man, Henry W. Grady, managing editor of the Atlanta *Constitution*, had emerged as the leading apostle of what Paul M. Gaston has called the New South creed, a tripartite program to restore prosperity and prominence to the region.[1]

Grady and other New South spokesmen believed that economic regeneration was the region's most pressing need. To effect this revival, they wished to solicit capital from wealthy Northern sources. The creed therefore proposed reconciliation between the old warring sections, North and South, and pointed to the many opportunities for good investments in the undeveloped region south of the Potomac.

To achieve sectional reconciliation, the creed promised an adjustment of the racial issue suitable to all concerned. Having repudiated slavery, New South spokesmen pledged to instruct the Negro in the ways of right living, to allow him the chance for an industrial education if he could secure the funds, and to respect the political rights he had won during Reconstruction. In return, the Negro had only to agree to abandon any claim to social equality with white Southerners, which he might feel his status as a free man gave him. What the renunciation of social equality meant, in effect, was that the Negro would have to occupy a separate, and perforce inferior, place in Southern society. This arrangement, New South spokesmen assured the North, was completely acceptable to the black man, who not only acquiesced in it but eagerly desired it. The New South creed proclaimed, moreover, that such a solution would eliminate the racial troubles of Reconstruction and would insure social stability, a quality highly prized by potential Northern investors.[2]

Racial accommodation and sectional reconciliation, then, would do much to guarantee the third part of the New South creed, an industrialized economy modeled on that of the North. It was this—industrialization—that was the be-all and end-all for Grady and the other men who led the New South movement.

They worked tirelessly. Preaching the new gospel in press and at podium, Grady alone made many converts, becoming, as John Donald Wade has written, "a hero all the way from Boston to Galveston." Southerners named their sons for him. Democrats mentioned him as a possible vice-presidential candidate. Even New York's New England Society greeted his "New South" address with unbridled enthusiasm.[3]

Other publicists echoed Grady's ideas: Richard H. Edmonds in Baltimore, Henry Watterson in Louisville, and Francis W. Dawson in Charleston, to name a few of the more prominent. For too long, they said, progress had bypassed the South. According to them, not only had the great war of 1861–65 killed the doctrine of secession, it had discredited forever the agricultural economy of the Old South. To the disciples of the New Order it was obvious that the North's more industrialized economy had been the major reason for the South's defeat. Why not learn a lesson from the conqueror, asked these men, emulate its economy, and bring the South into the mainstream of American life?[4]

New South spokesmen believed their region possessed two important prerequisites of an industrial economy: cheap labor and abundant natural resources. It seemed unnatural to New South advocates that the American textile industry should flourish in New England instead of the South where most of the nation's cotton was grown and that the blast furnaces of Pittsburgh should blaze unceasingly while the mineral wealth of the South lay unexploited in the ground. What the South lacked, these men said, was capital to develop its resources. Let the North supply this capital and everyone would be prosperous and satisfied. The South would build railroads to move the goods its new factories would produce, and idle Southerners would have jobs. Northern investors would realize fat profits, and the entire country would enjoy good times. There would, in short, be progress all around.[5]

The New South movement had wide appeal throughout the nation, often encompassing seemingly disparate elements. Former Abolitionists and Radical Republicans substituted avarice for moral zeal and together with Confederate veterans sought the goal of an industrialized South. Generals in gray who had once led Southern troops at Antietam and Gettysburg now worked on retainer for Jay Gould and other robber barons active in railroads branching into the South. Democratic politicians who had redeemed the South from Radical Reconstruction now clasped hands with Yankee Republicans and welcomed an invasion by Northern capital. These new alliances would work to transform Dixie much more thoroughly than the Radicals could ever have done.[6]

Northern aid usually meant a measure of Northern control of Southern business affairs. New South spokesmen nevertheless insisted that their movement was under the guidance of Southern men exclusively and pronounced the results of their efforts good. The accomplishments were considerable. The South was building cotton mills and blast furnaces. Its cities were growing. Railroads were penetrating hitherto isolated parts of the region. Still, the South remained the poorest section of the country, and in some economic indexes its position relative to the nation's was actually declining.[7]

The New South movement was creating its own mythology, however, and anyone attentive to the claims of its spokesmen would have doubted evidence of regional decline. The New South creed had undergone a metamorphosis: a program of action begun right after the war to lift up the depressed South had become by the late eighties a declaration of triumph depicting a South already enjoying the golden age of prosperity. The emphasis of the New South creed had changed from what could be done to what had been done. Just twenty-odd years after the Civil War, apostles of the New Order maintained that the New South movement had restored prosperity to a once-devastated land.[8]

If many Southerners believed in the myth of a prosperous, triumphant South, some remained skeptical. One such doubter was Lewis H. Blair of Richmond. In *The Prosperity of the South Dependent upon the Elevation of the Negro*, published in 1889, Blair, a well-to-do merchant and manufacturer from an old Virginia family, disputed the claims of New South spokesmen. Rather than the El Dorado pictured by these enthusiasts, most of the South, said Blair, was backward and poverty-ridden. He objected particularly to the way

New South publicists manipulated statistics. For instance, Richard H. Edmonds's inflated count of Southern factories included those existing only on paper and those once operating but since failed. Moreover, as Blair pointed out, a major business in the South, lumbering, was an extractive industry that helped the Southern economy only in the short run and did great harm to the region's natural resources. He showed that even the textile industry, the pride of the New South promoters, produced only coarse goods, leaving New England to manufacture the more profitable fine fabrics. Knowing that he invited the damnation of all good Southern patriots by daring to question the New South's pretensions, Blair nevertheless spoke frankly. The main reason for the region's lack of prosperity, he maintained, was the degradation of the Negro, a good source of labor but an element of the population largely neglected by the New South movement.[9]

Blair's criticisms looked to the future and were ahead of the times. Other detractors of the New South movement harked back to the past in their efforts to stem what they felt to be the rising tide of materialism. These traditional critics of the New South movement were often Confederate veterans of planter antecedents who had grown to manhood before the war and had a stronger allegiance to the antebellum South than did the apostles of change, most of whom were too young to have served in the Confederate army and were of urban, middle-class background. The traditionalists, in many ways ideological descendants of Thomas Jefferson and John Taylor of Caroline, upheld the agrarian ideal and deplored the New South's shrill cry for industrialization, which to them meant a capitulation to the crass materialism of Yankeedom.[10] Two such critics were especially conspicuous.

Robert L. Dabney, college professor, Presbyterian divine, and Stonewall Jackson's chief of staff, divided his intellectual labors between theological questions and attacks on the New South movement. He believed that change was inevitable and that wealth was essential to power, but he implored the South to resist materialism, to shun the North's example, to refuse "to make wealth the idol . . . of sectional greatness." To Dabney the "wisdom of the New South . . . [lay] in pursuing the sharp line which divides the neglect from the idolatry of riches." It was clear to him, however, that many of his contemporaries were ignoring that distinction.[11]

Another prominent traditional critic of the New South ideology was Charles C. Jones, Jr., of Georgia, the son of a Presbyterian minister, a lawyer and historian, and the perennial president of the Confederate Survivors Association. In his annual addresses before that body, Jones pilloried those heretics who knelt at "the shrine of Mammon" and who wanted to convert the South to a "money-worshipping domain." Like Dabney, Jones maintained that he had no quarrel with limited acquisitiveness. He thought he perceived in the South, however, a growing tendency to make money the mark of a man, and he raged against that trend. Believing Southerners to be a peculiar people, he exhorted them to remain so and asked God to grant "that this New South remain purged of all modern commercial methods."[12] Confronting the ideology of the New South movement head on, Jones stated his belief that "the truest test of civilization lies not in the census, in the growth of cities, in railway combinations and the formation of Gargantuan trusts, in the expansion of manufactures, in manipulation of land schemes and corporate securities, or in the aggregation of wealth, but in the mental, moral, political, and economic education and elevation of the population."[13] In his view the New South movement had failed to elevate the region's people and was merely enriching a few men in high places. Moreover, with Lewis Blair, Jones maintained that what prosperity the movement had achieved was grossly exaggerated; its extravagant claims were "largely a matter of imagination."[14]

For many of the South's more noteworthy creative writers, the initial response to the new dispensation was not so pat as the arguments advanced by both proponents and critics of the new ideology, sure of the rightness of their positions. In the earlier works of many of the writers, ambivalence rather than certainty characterized their attitude.

There were compelling reasons for Southern writers to support the new ideology. On a purely personal level, the Southern writer, after the unpleasantness of Reconstruction was over, usually depended on the North to sustain him, for Northerners, far more than Southerners, bought and read his works. During the period, virtually every Southern writer of note was discovered by the editors of such magazines as *Century*, *Lippincott's*, *Scribner's*, and even the staunchly Republican *Harper's Monthly* and *Atlantic Monthly*. The same houses that published these magazines often brought out Southern works in book form, too. The New South, then, by its ties to the North, opened doors to writers that had been closed before, so many of them set about exploiting the raw materials of literature just as the boomers tried to develop economic resources.[15] As William P. Trent noted in 1897, it would have been "a miracle of stupidity . . . if, in the . . . heyday of provincial literature the New South had missed the golden opportunity" to take advantage of local color and the Lost Cause.[16]

Southern writers were hardly stupid. They gave Yankee readers what they wanted: stories of the idyllic old plantation, tales of wartime valor, vignettes of exotic Creoles, portraits of picturesque mountaineers, and anything else unusual enough to arouse Northern interest.

Beyond merely professional considerations, Southern writers could feel the strong pull of the New South ideology. It offered hope amid despair, opportunity when for too long little had existed, the possibility of cultural attainment through material progress. The new ideology was, moreover, intellectually respectable; publicists, politicians, businessmen, and academicians espoused it. And the shapers of opinion assured skeptics that the South could industrialize without losing its distinctiveness, though they did not specify how.[17]

The New South professed to have no quarrel with the Old, for the magic of the Lost Cause, the source of its appeal to the North and to New South spokesmen, was that it was so irrevocably and satisfyingly lost. Now that Southern differences no longer threatened the Union, Yankees found them quaint and picturesque. North and South discovered much on which to agree: that the slaves had been happy, the masters kind, all Confederate soldiers brave, and Southern history a record of glory, even in defeat, or rather, especially in defeat. Accompanying the paeans to the past and often written by the same hands were fulsome prophecies of the South's bright future. Marvelously, many Southerners could memorialize the Old Order and at the same time tax its legacy by accepting the Northern way, the industrial ethic, as standard and admitting, at least tacitly by their very striving for Yankee favor, that the South had been deviant. The literature reflecting this way of thinking, much of it in the Plantation Tradition and artfully written by men such as Thomas Nelson Page and F. Hopkinson Smith, lent itself to sentimental romance that, by its bathetic treatment of the Old Order, offered no real alternative to the industrial, urban ethos. Often, in fact, the plantation romancers were quite effective propagandists for the New South movement.

Similar to the plantation romancers in their support of the New South movement were writers such as Thomas Dixon, Jr., and Will N. Harben who explicitly expounded the bourgeois ethic. Writers of this persuasion rejoiced in the coming of progress. If Dixon occasionally tried to force the bourgeois ethic into an uncomfortable alliance with the plantation myth, Harben would have none of that, attacking the old gentry savagely as, paradoxically, he infused his middle-class characters with virtues commonly considered aristocratic. Both writers welcomed the physical manifestations of the New Order: the construction of factories, the laying of railroad track, the growth of towns.

These proponents of the New South movement were simply adhering to the practice of their literary predecessors—the reinforcement of conventional values. For the antebellum writer the task had been to defend a civilization based on slavery. If he happened to oppose slavery, as did William Alexander Caruthers, he found it expedient to keep his views to himself.[18] As outside criticism of Southern civilization became the more strident, the more aggressive grew the defense. After 1830, Southerners believed themselves under siege. Manning the ramparts alongside the politicians and other proslavery apologists were the creative writers. The ideological and political debate between North and South insidiously affected the Southern writer by coaxing him, if he would be honored in his own land, to divert his energy into politics and polemics, to burden his art too heavily with argument. His inability to resist the strictures of the community blinded him to the blemishes of Southern society, kept him from relating much of the regional experience.

So it was with some postbellum writers, except that now orthodoxy meant acceding to, and portraying the merits of, the new prevailing ideology, the New South movement. Such writers, like their precursors in the Old South, reinforced establishmentarian values. And if the writer were someone like Thomas Nelson Page, able at the same time to draw so tenderly the features of the Old Order, then so much the better.

Yet if the "preachment of an alien ethics . . . went largely unchallenged" and was even endorsed by some Southern writers, quite a few of the more significant ones between Reconstruction and the First World War subscribed only temporarily, if at all, to the new ideology.[19] The more the New South movement gained the ascendancy, the more writers such as Paul Hamilton Hayne, John Esten Cooke, Sidney Lanier, Joel Chandler Harris, Mark Twain, George W. Cable, Charles W. Chesnutt, and Ellen Glasgow criticized and resisted it. Although there were great differences among some of these writers, underlying their opposition to the New Order was the common conviction that the South offered the reality, or at least the possibility, of arcadian alternative.[20]

With a long tradition in Southern letters, the pastoral image had helped fashion a belief in the South as a place where man drew the fullness of his humanity from the land; where leisure, though not indolence, was the ideal; where people lived, not merely made a living. To be sure, the postbellum plantation romancers drew upon this image, but in their hands it became simply nostalgic. Among some of the better writers, however, the arcadian ideal was a viable counterpoint to the Yankee way that massed men in physical proximity as it atomized them spiritually and emotionally. Unfettered acquisitiveness, to these writers a Yankee trait being imported by Grady and his ideological myrmidons, simply would not mesh with their notions of what made the South distinctive and appealing.

PART I

THE CURRENTS OF CHANGE: OLDER WRITERS AND THE NEW SOUTH MOVEMENT

I.

THE CAVALIER MANQUÉ:
THE NEW SOUTH MOVEMENT
FROM THE GEORGIA PINES

Paul Hamilton Hayne was one of a few established writers in the Old South whose career extended for many years into the postbellum period. Because he enjoyed a favored place in antebellum society and ardently defended the Southern way, the adjustment to postbellum conditions was especially painful for him. Perplexed by the New Order, he groped for a proper response, and for a time this son of the Old South tried to accommodate himself to the New South movement.

Few events illustrate the divided mind of Hayne and others of his generation better than the International Cotton Exposition of 1881. Eight thousand enthusiastic people, some of them prominent public men, came to the opening ceremonies in Atlanta's Oglethorpe Park to celebrate the restoration of King Cotton, to welcome the new heir apparent, Industrialism, and to gaze upon the thousand-odd exhibits designed to honor them.[1]

"The South's Great Show," the *New York Times* called the affair. Though attendance fell short of the promoters' hopes, for the exposition's three-month duration nearly 300,000 people came to see the latest methods and machinery for cotton growth and manufacture, innovations in rail transportation, and samples of the South's mineral resources. Compared with similar exhibitions occurring later, the great show of 1881 was unspectacular. Still, it was an early and impressive demonstration of the fervor of the New South movement. Conceived by a Northerner, directed by a Northerner, and financed to a considerable degree by Northern money, the exposition quickened the desire of many Southerners to develop an industrial economy and by its success encouraged Northern investors to send their money south.[2]

As Georgia's Governor Alfred H. Colquitt concluded his welcome and the opening ceremonies continued, Colonel N. J. Hammond rose to impart Southern literature's contribution to the occasion. This offering, "The Exposition Ode," was a poem praising the courage, industry, and perseverance of the people of Atlanta and the South and forecasting a glorious future for the New South. These verses celebrating the New Order came not from the pen of some young poet flush with the optimism of his years but from that of Paul Hayne, lingering Cavalier and singer of the virtues of the Old South. When Hammond finished the reading, the audience applauded enthusiastically.[3] No one, it seems, appreciated the irony.

Born into the Charleston gentry in 1830, Hayne, left fatherless as an infant, came early under the influence of his uncle, Robert Y. Hayne, just then becoming famous as the forensic adversary of Daniel Webster. As a boy, Paul Hayne attended Christopher Cotes's classical school and upon completing his studies there entered the College of Charleston from which he was graduated in 1850. Though a life in politics and the law beckoned, he became instead a man of letters. He found poetry his most congenial form of expression and early in life tried his hand at it, publishing his first poem when he was fifteen. By the outbreak of the Civil War, three volumes of his poetry were on the market, and he had served briefly as editor of *Russell's Magazine*, a Charleston literary periodical. In this capacity, he became closely associated with Henry Timrod and William Gilmore Simms and maintained that association until the end of their lives.[4]

The Civil War destroyed the good life Hayne had known. When sectional tensions erupted into open hostility, he joined the staff of Governor Francis W. Pickens. Poor health forced him to give up that duty in 1862, but he continued to serve the Confederacy with his pen, writing poems defending the Southern cause and urging his fellows to victory. Defeat came instead, and it was a bitter pill for Hayne. The Federal bombardment of Charleston had demolished his home and library. His native city now offered him little but unpleasant memories, so he moved with his family to a small tract of land he owned in the pine barrens of Georgia near Augusta. Here at Copse Hill, in a shanty papered with old magazines, he lived until his death in 1886, writing poems and fighting poverty and ill health.[5]

Despite his plight, Hayne never forsook the profession of letters for more lucrative work. Literature was his life, and he devoted his labors to it completely, writing reviews, biographical sketches, historical essays—and nearly 500 poems. It was in poetry that he established his reputation, and however diminished that reputation may be today, in his own time Hayne was known as the laureate of the South. Many of his poems deal with themes of nature, religious faith, home life, and classical mythology—in short, with romantic themes that would lend themselves to sentimentality in the hands of a writer such as Hayne, who lacked toughness and detachment. Only occasionally did he descend from his ethereal universe to treat mundane affairs.[6]

The bulk of Hayne's work shows that he thought of a poem as exclusively the vehicle for a beautiful sentiment finely expressed. A writer such as Walt Whitman who sang of sweat, sailors, and whores was not a poet at all, Hayne maintained, but a "prurient poetaster" whose ideas were "filthy and revolting."[7]

It was not that Hayne, the man, was unconcerned with contemporary affairs. A look at his correspondence, filled with splenetic remarks on postwar America, shows otherwise. He lamented the postbellum decline of the Southern planter class and the rise of the lower orders. He lashed out at the Radical Republicans of the North and their allies in the South for trying to reconstruct the region. He derided attempts to make a respectable place for Negroes in Southern society. He distrusted the ability of the "brute-born masses" to govern themselves and said that Jefferson and Madison had been wrong, for "republics are impossibilities!" From the seclusion of Georgia's pine barrens, he perceived the postwar world as too ugly to be poetic.[8]

Hayne's bitterness stemmed in part from his difficult personal situation and, the designation as the South's laureate notwithstanding, from the relative neglect he suffered as a writer. He saw himself as a poet without honor in America and even in his native Southland. Remarking to friends that the South was a cultural wasteland, he bemoaned its fawning over second-rate politicians and its lack of concern for men of letters. Dismay over his treatment by Southerners caused him to envy his literary friends in the North who enjoyed a more appreciative audience.[9] Sometimes he even acted obsequiously toward these acquaintances. The good gray poets of New England—John Greenleaf Whittier, Oliver Wendell Holmes, Henry Wadsworth Longfellow, and James Russell Lowell—he considered giants of American literature. He praised even their poorer works lavishly and wrote verses in their honor.[10] Because he longed for recognition from his peers, the earlier association of some of these poets with abolitionism seemed to bother the old defender of slavery very little.

Notwithstanding Hayne's regret over what the North had done to the South, his friendly relations with some Northern editors and poets led him occasionally to support the growing efforts for sectional reconciliation. He congratulated Longfellow on his memorial to President Garfield and hoped that it would help bring North and South closer together. Moreover, any extraordinary show of kindness by the North to the South, such as the relief sent New Orleans during the epidemic of yellow fever in 1878, moved Hayne to express generous sentiments toward the old adversary. Such expressions were exceptions to his prevailing attitude of hostility, however, and continuing to denounce the North's politics and society, he preferred usually to confine his relations with that section to literary matters.[11]

The mood of sectional reconciliation was ascendant, though, and this feeling together with a sense of regional pride prompted Southerners to stage great agricultural and industrial fairs and commemorations of historical events during the 1880s. The fairs, such as the Atlanta exposition, brought the sections together in praise of the present and in hope for the future. The historical celebrations, such as the centennials of the battles at King's Mountain and at Yorktown, encouraged Americans to remember and appreciate their common heritage of resistance to British tyranny.

Regardless of Hayne's protests of neglect at Southern hands, he was in considerable demand as an occasional poet, and the managers of these three great celebrations of the eighties asked him to write verses appropriate to the ceremonies. He complied willingly. It was hardly unusual for the defender of the antebellum South to honor the requests of the celebrants of King's Mountain and Yorktown and consent to praise his region's past. He had done this before without solicitation. In light of his frequently expressed distaste for the New Order, however, it is puzzling that he would agree to compose a poem for an exposition lauding the New South. Perhaps he felt duty-bound to comply with a request from his adopted state of Georgia. No doubt, too, he was grateful for the recognition accorded him by prominent men. To someone of his limited resources, moreover, the promised payment of $100 for his contribution was no small consideration. Whatever the reasons, Hayne, it seems, saw nothing inconsistent in writing an encomium to the New Order.[12]

A long poem of more than 200 lines with irregular rhyme scheme and complex metrical and stanzaic forms, "The Exposition Ode" follows the style of Hayne's earlier works with its sometimes careless grammatical usage, abundant allusions to classical mythology, and dreamy quality (the poem is framed in a vision). There is, however, a major difference between this composition and many of Hayne's other poems, the themes of which are alien to life in the South. The theme of "The Exposition Ode" comes directly out of Southern experience.

The poem records the postwar history of Atlanta through the observations of the poet-narrator whose moods, like those of the city he describes, pass from shock over military defeat, through despair over Atlanta's abject state, toward hope for a better future through hard work, and finally to triumph, a victory proclaimed by an admiring nation. Divided into three major parts, the "Ode" begins with a description of Atlanta before the exposition, then deals with the fair itself, and concludes with Hayne's predictions for the future.

As depicted at war's end, Atlanta's condition is pathetic. Conquered by "alien lords," "ravished and o'erthrown," "unrobed, discrowned," she reminds the poet of a mythological princess.[13]

> A new Andromeda, beside the main
> Of her own passionate pain;
> Bowed, naked, shivering low—
> Veils the soft gleam of melancholy eyes.
> Yet lovelier in their woe,—
> Alike from hopeless earth and hopeless skies.[14]

Yet, unlike Andromeda, Atlanta has no Perseus to rescue her, though finally she needs no outside savior. For as the poet describes her,

> This city of our love
> Is no poor, timorous dove,
> To crouch and die unstruggling in the mire. . . .[15]

Relying upon "that dauntless hardihood / Drawn to her veins from out the iron hills," the city rises, clasping "her old belief, / In God

and goodness," "trusting only to her strong right arm" to over-
come adversity.[16]

From this point on, the "Ode" chronicles Atlanta's, and by extension the South's, successes. "War-wasted lands . . . Flush into
golden harvests prodigal"; busy merchants signal the revival of
trade; railways carry goods to distant parts. The resurgence culmi-
nates with the summons to the great exposition, "a glorious festi-
val / Of art and commerce," called out of a desire for sectional
reconciliation, "for sweet sisterhood" in the bond "Blissful and
fond, / That yet may hold all nations in its thrall."[17]

The lines describing the exposition itself are given over entirely
to admiring the South's agricultural produce. Although grain elic-
its tender lines, cotton calls forth the poet's warmest tribute.

> But piled o'er all, thro' many an unbound bale
> Peering to show its snow-white softness pale,
> —Snow-white, yet warm, and destined to be furled
>   In some auspicious day,
>   For which we yearn and pray,
> Round half the naked misery of the world,
> A fleece more rich than Jason's, glances down.[18]

Having praised the product providing the fair's theme, Hayne
envisions Atlanta's future in the final section. Acknowledging that

> The years unborn
> Doubtless must bring to thee
> Trials to test thy spirit's constancy[19]

he nevertheless affirms the city's ultimate triumph, made the more
glorious for being heralded by the rest of the world. Atlanta's
destiny is, above all else, "heaven's purpose perfected."[20]

> Thou, nobly pure,
> Of any darkening taint of selfish greed,—
>   Wert pre-ordained to be
>   Purveyor of divinest charity,—
> The love-commissioned almoner of God.[21]

One student of Hayne's poetry has called "The Exposition Ode"
"eloquent and enthusiastic," a fit companion to Grady's famous
"New South" oration of 1886.[22] A casual reading of the poem does
indicate that Hayne was indeed endorsing fully the belief in prog-

ress held by New South spokesmen. Like the region's promoters, he exaggerates Southern resources. Atlanta reigns "midmost a large and opulent store, / Of all things wrought to meet a nation's need."[23] Like the boomers, he transforms a hopeful program of action into a declaration of triumph largely by wishful thinking. Like New South spokesmen, he insists that the region can win progress without capitulating to materialism. Atlanta is "High-souled to gain. . . The matchless splendor of Toil's 'golden fleece!'"[24] In all probability it was Hayne's conscious intention to extol material progress. Yet if we look closely at the poet's use of language, particularly at the imagery he employs, we can find elements contradictory to his design.

Hayne was above all else a poet of nature, and, to him, nature ideally was kind, gentle, feminine. Despite the occasionally forceful tone of "The Exposition Ode," it is informed by his use of natural and feminine imagery, and as a result its overall effect is one of gentleness. The section depicting the exposition itself omits any reference to the mechanical contrivances, agents of power, that were the fair's major attraction. The protagonist of the poem, the city of Atlanta, is personified as a woman. Though displaying great fortitude in overcoming her abject condition, the heroine Atlanta, resurgent at last, "Just rounding to rare curves of womanhood," retains the qualities of idealized femininity: beauty, sweetness, generosity.[25] This picture of postwar Atlanta tells us more about Hayne than it does about the city itself. Hayne consciously believed in the Cavalier ideal of exalted womanhood, and when he depicted Atlanta in this tradition he bestowed the highest praise he could offer. A personification of Atlanta truer to life would have likened the bustling little city to a young man, not a woman, out to make a name for himself, aggressive and headstrong, with an eye on the main chance. But to Hayne such qualities were hardly praiseworthy, so he would not invest an object he wished to honor with them.

In addition to this romantic picture of Atlanta, Hayne's vision of the New South in "The Exposition Ode" attempts to reconcile material progress with the pastoral ideal. In the South of the poet's imagination, summer flowers festoon the railway lines, and prosperity lives metaphorically as a green-leaved, majestic tree. But railroad tracks had to be kept clear of vegetation, and less poetic promoters of the New South envisioned prosperity more in the form of a cotton mill than a majestic tree. Near the end of the poem, Hayne also describes Atlanta itself in natural imagery. He portrays the city as a sort of earth goddess, innocent of her old implements of war and girded now to defend bloodlessly the cause of progress,

> Thy spear a fulgent shaft of sun-steeped grain;
> Thy shield a buckler, the field-fairies wove
> Of strong green grasses, in the silvery noon
> Of some full harvest-moon,
> Thy stainless crown, red roses, blent with white![26]

The Atlanta of the poet's vision, pastoral and gentle, in harmony with nature, bears little resemblance to the booming little city already committed to the exploitation rather than the preservation of nature.

If Hayne's infelicitous image of postwar Atlanta casts doubt upon his understanding of the New South movement, his description of one aspect of the New South, industrialization—found in the first section where he is setting the stage for a depiction of the exposition itself—employs language more appropriate to the subject treated. Read in context, the brief passage on industrialization is just another item in the poet's catalogue of the New South's achievements. But the difference between these lines and many of the others is significant and shows both the fascination and the fear Hayne had of the machine's raw power.

> Set by the steam-god's fiery passion free,
> I hear the rise and fall
> Of ponderous iron-clamped machinery,
> Shake, as with earthquake thrill, the factory halls;
> While round the massive walls
> Slow vapor, like a sinuous serpent steals—
> Through which revolve in circles, great or small,
> The deafening thunders of the tireless wheels![27]

In this passage the poet again uses natural imagery, but he associates industrialism with a different kind of nature. Absent are the allusions to a gentle nature of grain, grass, and flowers. Instead, nature in these lines, is strong, violent, destructive, even sinister. The references to fire, earthquake, vapor, thunder, the steam-god, and the serpent make one feel that the machine was designed by the devil and erupted from the very bowels of hell. What effect would such unfettered energy have on the South of Hayne's dreams? How could the poet hope to preserve the South of benign and gentle nature against such a force? The serpent had entered the garden. Hayne saw its coming, he described it, and yet he failed here to protest it.

The question, then, is why did this admirer of an edenic South acquiesce in and even praise the coming of the machine? Hayne believed, as "The Exposition Ode" shows, that the seemingly great rejuvenation of the South was exclusively the work of Southerners. Upon advance receipt of the poem, the managers of the exposition had complained that, considering the great fair's design, the piece did not have a sufficiently national flavor, that it dealt too much with Atlanta and the South, and that it failed to develop the theme of sectional reconciliation to a suitable degree. Hayne refused to make any changes.[28] He failed even to delete the implicit analogy of the victorious North to the sea monster bent on destroying Andromeda (Atlanta). What this refusal demonstrates is that Hayne by his own lights was intensely loyal to the South. Above all else, he wanted to see the South respected in the eyes of the world. Anything, including the machine, that would restore his land to prominence he would welcome, as long as he could satisfy himself that the South would accomplish this restoration on its own, without the help of the arrogant North.

Hayne insisted, however, that the South, in the rush for riches and renown, cleave to its past and refuse to repudiate it to gain the favor of others. As it became increasingly apparent to him that the New South's professed reverence for the Old South lacked substance, his disaffection with the New South movement grew. He could still boast—as in the "Lyric" for Louisville's Southern Exposition of 1883—of the natural wealth of his region. But no longer did his poetry welcome industrialization, for he had come to believe that the machine produced more than material goods. To him it generated among Southerners a disrespect for the agrarian tradition of the antebellum South, no matter how much the postwar South might protest to the contrary.

Hayne showed his disillusionment with this development in a sonnet published in 1885 which bears quoting in its entirety:

To the New South

New South! new South! we hail your radiant rise
The morning sunshine flasht across your crest,
Your eagle-wings and proudly-swelling breast,
The soul that burns and brightens in your eyes,
But while you dare to storm the loftiest skies,
Foul not the fairness of your natal nest,
Nor in high Orient soaring scorn the West,
Wherein your Fathers' sunset glory lies:

How oft is sunset beautiful and grand!
Its very clouds are steeped in light and grace,
The glow and pathos of a farewell time—
'Tis thence the Past uplifts her dying face,
—And if that Past hath been like *ours* sublime,
Oh! Show her reverence in the Sunset-land![29]

The poet's emphasis here is unmistakable, and it is clear where his loyalty lies. In his eyes the fragile and dying past is immeasurably finer than the radiant and vigorous present. Though the first four lines of the octave pay tribute to the New South, the remainder of the poem glorifies the past and entreats the postwar South to cherish it. The poet suspects, however, that the New South considers other matters more pressing.

Elsewhere, Hayne extolled "the antique virtues of a worthier day," deplored the "growing tendency towards contempt for the Past, & a truckling spirit, so far as Yankee ideas, & Yankee prejudices are concerned," and lamented "the annihilation of our [Southern] Civilization, . . . the only conservative force in America."[30] In a plea that surely came from the heart, he admonished Southerners, in one of his last poems, to "be loyal still / To the sacred and stainless Past!"[31] Hayne, then, abandoned accommodation to the new ideology in favor of resistance. Adrift in the uncharted waters of a strange New South, he had, finally, his view of the South's past as a mooring for mind and spirit.

II.

THE WORK ETHIC AND
THE PASTORAL IDEAL:
JOHN ESTEN COOKE'S
HEIR OF GAYMOUNT

As Paul Hayne was lost spiritually and intellectually in the New South, so was his contemporary, John Esten Cooke. The similarities between the men are many: each was born in 1830 and died in 1886; each was of good family; each forsook the law for literature; each served the Confederate cause, Cooke in the field for four years; each defended in his work the Southern Cavalier tradition; and each attempted to come to terms with the New Order and, finally, could not.

Cooke's first composition was a poem, but subsequently he turned to fiction, producing much of it during the fifties. Devoting his labors to the subject most appealing to his imagination, colonial Virginia on the eve of the American Revolution, he fashioned his finest novel, *The Virginia Comedians*.[1]

As a young writer in the Old South, Cooke was a complex figure. He lamented the cult of progress of the nineteenth century, feared what it would do to Virginia, and tried to escape spiritually into the past. Colonial Virginia as he treats it is both a metaphor for the rural life and agrarian values he prized and a retreat from the "corrosive smoke issuing from the industrial stacks of Richmond." At the same time, however, Cooke appreciated the material benefits progress would bring to his cherished Virginia. He believed, moreover, that only through economic advance could Virginia regain the enviable position it held in the days of Washington and Jefferson. It was this conviction and his love for his state that enabled Cooke to resolve the debate in his own mind. If progress could be brought to Virginia by Virginians and not by outsiders, then he would welcome it. Still, Cooke maintained that prosperity could come without too much industrialization and urbanization;

and even in the postwar years, as the cry for industries swelled, he held to that belief.[2]

The Heir of Gaymount, the fictional formulation of Cooke's creed, complemented the ideas of some other men. Although the program designed to rebuild the South through industrialization had its genesis in the immediate postbellum years, many of the earliest advocates of a New South, having grown up in the agrarian society of the Old South, looked to agriculture as the best means to effect the region's economic redemption. These men held no brief for the staple-crop economy of the antebellum South, however, for they had seen King Cotton handled roughly by the stronger and more versatile economy of the North. Instead, their program for regional restoration concentrated on diversifying the South's farm products. For example, Daniel Harvey Hill of North Carolina advised Southern farmers to depend less on cotton, to grow more vegetables and fruits and to rotate the planting of them, to use fertilizers to enrich the soil, and generally to educate themselves in the methods of scientific farming.[3]

Though men such as Hill welcomed manufacturing, they wanted it to supplement, not to supplant, diversified farming as the basis of the region's economy. In such a design, they believed, lay the salvation of the postwar South. Its economy would be more self-sufficient; its soil would recover its fertility; its people would remain on the land, maintaining that moral superiority reserved to agricultural societies.[4]

Cooke was a fervent defender of agrarian values, as *The Heir of Gaymount* shows. The action of the story occurs in Virginia's Northern Neck from 1865 to 1868. The main character, Edmund Carteret, is a Confederate veteran of proud stock who is heir to the old plantation of Gaymount, reduced now after the war to a mere forty acres. In the early part of the story, Edmund's financial condition is so desperate that he considers selling his land and joining Maximilian's forces in Mexico. Upon reflection, however, he decides to stay and face his problems, the major one being to save his land from the tax collector. Just as the taxes are due, Frank Lance, a Northern friend whom Edmund met during the war, arrives at Gaymount. Learning of his friend's plight, Lance insists that Carteret accept payment for a wartime favor. Edmund reluctantly agrees, pays the taxes, and saves Gaymount for the time being.

Meantime, Edmund renews an acquaintance with Annie Vawter,

a childhood playmate, and falls in love with her. He learns that her father is being plagued by one Israel Tugmuddle, a former overseer at Gaymount turned usurer. Holding a debt of Major Vawter's, Tugmuddle suggests that he will cancel it if the major will let Annie marry his son. Major Vawter angrily rejects the offer, although he knows he may lose his home, the Reeds, by doing so. To save the Reeds from the auctioneer's hammer, Edmund offers Gaymount as security for Vawter's place. Tugmuddle then secures the bond on Gaymount, which must be paid within two years or the property will become his.

The prospect of Tugmuddle's living in the ancestral home of the Carterets spurs Edmund to act. He had already begun to farm his forty acres, and now he works even more vigorously to save Gaymount from the man who had ruined his father by chicanery. Following the advice of his friend Lance, Edmund engages in diversified farming. By cutting the trees in the park and plowing up the old racing turf, he uses every available acre for crops. He plants grains, vegetables, and a grape arbor. The grapes are his pride, and he expects that their wine will furnish a good living to himself and Annie, who is now his wife. Gaymount lacks the grandness of former years, but, as Cooke has young Carteret say, it rests on a much firmer financial foundation.

Edmund is doing well indeed. In two years of truck farming, he earns a net profit of $9,000 and saves $6,000 of his income. The prospect of paying off the bond on Gaymount, due in thirty days, is good. At this juncture, however, ill fortune intervenes in the person of a bank employee who absconds with Edmund's savings. It appears now that Gaymount will fall to Tugmuddle, but Carteret is heartened by a dissipated, dying cousin, who tells him of a will drawn by their uncle leaving much more of the Carteret estate than Gaymount to Edmund. Young Carteret's hopes are short-lived, though, when it appears he cannot find the will. Again, fortune, this time benevolent, intercedes. Pecking about Gaymount, Annie's pet swan uncovers a scrap of paper. The paper contains a coded message, which, after due effort, Edmund deciphers. The message directs him to a chest buried on the grounds of Gaymount. Upon opening the chest, Edmund finds not only the will but the family plate and coins and bank notes in abundance. Now the owner of all the Carteret lands, Edmund foils Tugmuddle, pays the bond on Gaymount, and looks happily to a bright future.

The Heir of Gaymount may be read not only as a novel but as a treatise on scientific agriculture. Cooke himself was farming in 1868 when he wrote the book, and he knew whereof he spoke.[5] At various points he describes the methods of correct farming in considerable detail. After Edmund has secured the proper implements, he breaks ground; then he drains a nearby swamp and fires the brush so that the ashes will reduce the acidity of the land. He also plants clover to enrich the soil in certain parts of the tract. He is careful to use the correct fertilizers in the right amounts, and he prepares beds from which he transplants the shoots to the fields. When Edmund's friend Lance asks him why other farmers in Virginia lag in diversifying their crops, Edmund replies that they are captives of the old ways. Their fathers and grandfathers planted only staple crops, so that must be right. They fail to realize, he says, that staple crops require more land than many farmers, their acreage reduced by the war, possess. Agriculture in Virginia is behind the times, Edmund affirms, and he likens its state of development to "running a stage line along the railway."[6]

No one can accuse Edmund of being behind the times. He is a progressive farmer. Tilling the soil is a business to him, and Cooke extols his businesslike demeanor. An energetic man, Edmund objects to being considered a "worthless, stuck-up, sham, 'gentleman.'" When Lance exclaims that Edmund's bustle and hard work contradict the common image of the proper Virginian, Edmund replies that work is the only thing that will rebuild the South. He admits that he is out to turn a profit, for "profit means prosperity, and prosperity means churches, lyceums, academies, schools, railroads, material advancement and happiness." If Southerners desire these things, they must work hard, save their money, and stay out of debt. Begin on a small scale, Edmund learns, and a larger structure can be fashioned in time.[7]

Edmund embodies a curious blend of the work ethic and the pastoral ideal. He has a deep-seated love of the land. When he extols the virtues of labor, he means labor in the earth, not in factories. Nowhere in the novel is there mention of industrialization—as if Cooke wished to ignore its existence. Urban life receives its share of attention and abuse, however. Lance describes Gotham (New York) as a place "where bulls and bears are fighting in Wall Street [and] where people are getting run over on Broadway." In an authorial observation, Cooke himself portrays cities as "omnivorous, and greedy of what nature offers." Producing little of true value, cities feed off the beneficence of the land and are consequently morally inferior to agricultural societies.[8]

Carteret's love of the land and pride in his heritage make him something of a traditionalist, notwithstanding his criticisms of the Old South's staple-crop economy. When Lance notices the Carteret family tree on the wall at Gaymount, he good-naturedly chides Edmund for presuming "under the sun of the nineteenth century to possess . . . a *grandfather!*" Lance also, with tongue in cheek, scores Virginia for "lagging far behind the grand civilization of the nineteenth century." Edmund, however, holds to his belief that Virginia's past is a thing of substance as opposed to the "new varnish and gilt gingerbread" of their own time.[9]

In *The Heir of Gaymount* Cooke had chosen the kind of subject dear to later literary realists, a subject grounded in the here and now, in the daily existence of an average human being. But he treated a realistic theme in the fashion of sentimental romanticism. Horatio Alger could have been proud of the plot: a young man of fine character but straitened circumstances struggles to rise in the world, marries the girl of his dreams, and through luck and pluck overcomes all obstacles, grows prosperous, and lives happily ever after. The plot, moreover, depends upon stock romantic devices for resolution: clumsy coincidences, coded messages, buried treasure. As in much of the fiction of the time, there is also a sentimental love story, though Cooke at least had the good sense and ability to tie it directly to plot development. If the plot is flawed, so are the characters, who are not so much people as types. Present are the fallen but struggling aristocrat, the sweet and beautiful maiden, the villainous low white, and the faithful old darky.

The unrealistic handling of material was a legacy of the antebellum literary dispensation under which Cooke had learned his craft. Though his subject was pertinent to contemporary affairs, a quality often missing in the fiction of the Old South, his technique had changed little. The aristocratic impulse remained strong: one's standing in polite society determined his worth as a human being. And there was no one else quite as worthy as a Virginia planter. Cooke therefore could not let Carteret stay a truck farmer. He had to restore him to his antebellum position.

Notwithstanding the many faults of *The Heir of Gaymount*, its composition cost Cooke much labor. He was later to return to the kind of writing—mainly historical romances of revolutionary Virginia—he could do more easily.[10] For a time shortly after 1865, however, Cooke felt he had something of direct relevance to say to Virginia and, by extension, to the entire South. His prescription was a mixture of progress and tradition. Though he later voiced his conviction that "advance should be the law," he hoped the South's advance would conserve and perpetuate its agrarian heritage.[11] Industrialization might bring material progress, but it would also bury the South's past. An economy based on diversified agriculture would preserve the region's agrarian society, and if properly managed, this economy could also bring prosperity. The South, then, would have the best of both worlds. She would grow rich like the North, yet she would remain a distinctive land morally superior to the urban, industrial society above the Potomac.

Few Southerners heeded Cooke's call for conservative change. It is ironic that a novel by one of the South's most popular writers went unread. Most Southern farmers continued to plant staple crops, and the younger leaders of the New South movement emphasized industrializaton rather than an economy based on diversified agriculture. But, as a practical matter, what rejoinder could Cooke make? On his own farm, where he tried to do some of the things Edmund Carteret did, he was forced to supplement his income from the soil by writing.[12]

The subject matter of *The Heir of Gaymount* failed to fire Cooke's imagination, and he admitted as much.[13] Creatively, he was more absorbed with the past than with the present, although he knew the costs of his predilection. As he wrote shortly before his death, "Mr. Howells and the other realists have crowded me out of popular regard as a novelist, and have brought the kind of fiction I write into general disfavor. I do not complain of that, for they are right. They see, as I do, that fiction should faithfully reflect life, and they obey the law, while I can not. I was born too soon, and am now too old to learn my trade anew."[14]

He was also too old to learn a new creed. To him, a Southern alliance with the Northern way meant the abandonment of the South's distinctive heritage. He came to believe that the New South's blindness to the region's golden past resulted from gazing uncritically upon the gilded civilization above the Potomac.

PART II

THE SOUTH RESURGENT: LITERARY PROPONENTS OF THE NEW SOUTH MOVEMENT

III.

THE BEST OF ALL POSSIBLE WORLDS:
THE PLANTATION TRADITION AND
THE NEW SOUTH MOVEMENT

When Cooke and Hayne died in 1886, a literary genre that had flourished in antebellum America was returning with even more impact than it had exerted before the war. Exemplars of Southern gentility, Hayne and Cooke would doubtless have been pleased with the resurgence of plantation romance and its hegemony over readers of belles lettres from the late eighties on. Yet they would hardly have countenanced a purpose for which that writing was used—the reinforcement of the New South movement.

One function of antebellum plantation romance as written by John Pendleton Kennedy, William Gilmore Simms, Cooke himself, and others of less talent had been to picture the South as edenic and orderly and the North as philistine and chaotic, to present the Cavalier ideal as a viable counterpoise to the Yankee way.[1] By contrast, postbellum plantation romance, because it dealt with a relic, had no vital alternative to champion. That literature was instead nostalgia pure and simple, catering to an outside audience that found plantation society merely picturesque. By necessity then, if not choice, postbellum romance implicitly and explicitly promoted the industrial ethic, though disguising its message in the trappings of tradition.

The common element among writers of the Plantation Tradition was the portrayal of the Southern plantation as the peculiar setting for the good life. Into their romantic rendering of life among the gentry went various ingredients: the columned mansion; the expansive lawn graced with trees and flowers; the broad, fecund acres; the old planter, the embodiment of virtuous manliness; the mistress, dreamlike in her aloofness and commanding the respect of all; the young cavalier, hot-blooded and quick to anger but withal a good fellow; the young belle, always beautiful and usually spirited; the banjo-picking darky, happy and grateful for the good fortune of security without responsibility; the old uncle, wise in the ways of man and nature and honored even by his white superiors; and the mammy, strong and fiercely protective of her white charges.[2]

Although such a life and the literature depicting it were romantic enough before the Civil War, the destruction of that life in 1865 caused plantation romancers to compensate for its loss by describing it in terms even more unreal. That is to say, the postbellum Plantation Tradition was enlarged, embellished, embroidered, and placed at even greater distance from actuality than its predecessor. By the 1880s, "all restraints were declared off and the romancers of plantation life were allowed any measure of romantic abandon."[3]

That the plantation as a functioning reality no longer existed made glorification of it harmless, or so many people thought. Indeed, as Southerners soon learned, the Plantation Tradition and the legend of the Lost Cause worked to reinforce each other and to fashion a view of Southern history quite helpful in changing outside opinion of the South. As C. Vann Woodward has written, "One of the most significant inventions of the New South was the 'Old South'—a new idea in the eighties, and a legend of incalculable potentialities."[4]

Few writers in the Plantation Tradition could equal Thomas Nelson Page and F. Hopkinson Smith. When in 1892 these men opened a reading tour in Boston, they regaled audiences in the old Abolitionist stronghold for four days with tales of the old plantation. Page read his stories "Marse Chan" and "Meh Lady" as he had written them, in the dialect of the old-time darkies. Smith delivered passages from his recently published novel, *Colonel Carter of Cartersville*, in the rolling syllables of the title character himself. From Boston they traveled to New York, Chicago, Philadelphia, Baltimore, and Washington and were received at each performance with enthusiastic and sustained applause. They were superb; the audiences roared for more.[5]

The postbellum invention of the legendary Old South, on which Page and Smith held patents and which captivated even Bostonians, was not fashioned by design. Few people thought of calculating the tangible benefits of the Old South to the New. The creation of the mythic Old South was rather the stuff men live by. It gave Southerners something to cling to, to take pride in. Though defeated, they could look back to glory and forward to the promise of revival. For, paradoxically, the Old South created in the Plantation Tradition complemented and gave sustenance to the New South movement.[6]

Southerners claimed to see continuity between the Old and the New. Henry Grady, the new spirit made flesh, said that the postwar South was "simply the Old South under new conditions."[7] Thomas Nelson Page, the supreme glorifier of the old regime, believed that "the New South is . . . simply the Old South with its energies directed into new lines."[8] Both men refused to acknowledge that these new conditions and redirected energies—primarily the movement toward industrialization—might make the offspring unrecognizable to the progenitor. Like revolutionaries who "anxiously conjure up the spirits of the past to their service and borrow from them," each man sought to bind the New Order to the Old.[9] The tie was dextrously made, but the bond was loose.

When "Marse Chan" was published in 1884, it fairly thrust its author, Thomas Nelson Page, upon the national literary stage. The circumstances of his life, many readers felt, peculiarly suited him to memorialize the plantation society of old Virginia. Born in 1853 at Oakland, his family's estate in Hanover County, Page was descended from two of the leading houses of the Old Dominion. Both the Page and the Nelson families had been in Virginia for more than a century and had figured prominently in the state's history. They lived as country gentlemen and accepted both the perquisites and the responsibilities of their position.

Although the Civil War and Reconstruction disrupted the course of events at Oakland, Page was still able to enter Washington College in 1869. He failed to take a degree, however, and worked for a short time as a tutor, an occupation he considered demeaning to someone of his social background. Resuming his formal education, he completed the law course at the University of Virginia and began practicing law on the Hanover circuit. But the lure of the city soon proved too strong to resist, and two years later, in 1876, he moved to Richmond to work for an uncle who was counsel for the Chesapeake and Ohio Railway. This descendant of the plantation gentry found both working for the railroad and life in the city appealing.[10]

Page had begun to try his hand at writing as a student, having composed pieces for journals at Washington College and at the university in Charlottesville.[11] As he settled into urban life, he discovered a subject for his literary impulse. Now that he had in reality distanced himself from the environment of his youth, he turned in his fancy to that world and proceeded to wrap it in a romantic shroud that still clings to it. His first well-known composition was a poem in Negro dialect, "Uncle Gabe's Christmas," modeled on Irwin Russell's "Christmas Night in the Quarters." By 1887, when his stories of the old regime were collected in *In Ole Virginia*, Page, at the forefront of the plantation romancers, had put the writers of anti-Southern persuasion in full retreat.[12]

Largely on the strength of *In Ole Virginia*, some students of Page have equated his nostalgia for the Old Order with hostility toward the New South.[13] The contrast is forced and exists more in the minds of the critics than in the author himself. Page's contemporaries were not thus misled. Though they failed, as did Page, to perceive the real discontinuity between the Old and the New, they saw in his stories little to hurt and much to help the New South movement.

A key element in much postbellum literature is the idea of sectional reconciliation, and Page's plantation romances are no exception.[14] In "Meh Lady," for instance, he resolves the plot by marrying the Southern belle to the Federal officer, the joining of these individuals standing for the reunion of the sections.[15] A similar resolution—and the promise of another—occurs in *Red Rock*, his novel of Reconstruction. In Page's works, moreover, reconciliation takes place on the South's terms. The well-meaning Northern characters with errant views toward the South eventually revise their misconceptions and become good Southerners themselves.

The sine qua non in the conversion process was to embrace the conventional Southern doctrine on the race question. No volume of legislation could make the black man the equal of the white, Page maintained, and such efforts only aggravated the tense racial situation in the South. He believed the Negro Problem would be greatly reduced were the destiny of the black man left to his best friend and guardian, the Southern white man. The white South would dispel from black Southerners any notions of equality and would insure that blacks remained in their proper place of subservience where, after all, they were much more content.[16] Believing sectional reconciliation and the semblance of racial harmony essential to securing the Northern capital needed for industrialization, New South spokesmen could second Page's proposals heartily.

There are other instances of agreement between Page and men more commonly thought of as advocates of a New South. In "Marse Chan" the author is careful to portray the hero as a Unionist who disapproves of secession and fights in the Confederate army only to defend his native soil. Page illustrates his belief that the Old South was the stronghold of nationalism, that the noblest Southerners were proud to be Americans, and that Abolitionists and Fire-eaters eliminated sectional accommodation and drove moderate men to secession only as a last recourse. This view fit snugly with that of New South spokesmen, for whom the true Southern heritage was the tradition of Virginian nationalism rather than the legacy of Carolinian sectionalism.[17]

Page's long and limping novel, *Red Rock*, belongs to the same period of his literary career as *In Ole Virginia*. Although the novel was not published until 1898, the author had written it and revised it at least once by 1885.[18] A conventional story of Reconstruction, *Red Rock* contains the usual assortment of carpetbaggers, scalawags, and misguided blacks on one side, and on the other, genteel, brave, and long-suffering Southern whites. In the course of the narrative, Page touches tangentially upon such aspects of the New South as railroad construction and economic development of Southern resources, treating these themes ambivalently. For example, he contrasts businessmen unfavorably with the old Southern gentlemen who seldom think of material matters. But even though the new dispensation receives an abundance of abuse, it should be remembered that business is described in terms of Reconstruction. That is, the promoters of railroads and the developers of resources are unscrupulous Northern capitalists, carpetbaggers, or scalawags.

Although the older Southern gentlemen have little interest in business matters, this is not the case with some of the younger Southerners of the novel. Jacquelin Gray, a Confederate veteran and heir to the plantation of Red Rock, wants to see changes made in the postwar South that will bring it into the mainstream of American life. But he is forced from this position by the Radical Republicans who have usurped control of the South's economy for their own ends rather than for the good of the region.[19] Reconstruction, then, in Page's view is vicious not only because it desecrates the memory of the Old South but also because it impedes progress for the New South. The corrupt Radicals keep energetic young Southerners such as Gray from leading their region out of depression into prosperity. The implication is clear: once Reconstruction has ended, the South can conduct its own economic regeneration—with the help of Northern capital, to be sure, but without the interference of dishonest and disruptive elements.

Page's main purpose in Red Rock was both to defend the South's resistance to Reconstruction and to pay homage to the Old South. Disgusted at what he perceived to be the attitude of his contemporaries toward the Old Order, Page believed, as he stated in the preface of the novel, that "Every ass that passes by kicks at the dead lion."[20] Whether he wrote that opinion in 1885 or in 1898, he was mistaken. The dead lion of the Lost Cause, rather than a carcass to be trampled, had by then become an idol for all to worship. And Page, in cooperation with Grady and associates, had helped to construct the shrine.

Neither man saw inconsistency in his position. In the spring of 1888 Grady invited Page to give a reading for the Piedmont Chautauqua, another of Grady's promotions at Salt Springs near Atlanta. Page accepted, appearing that summer to read "Unc' Edinburg's Drowndin'," a sentimental story of master-slave relations in old Virginia. His performance was the highlight of the season. The Georgia air was filled with nostalgia for the Old South and enthusiasm for the New, and the elements blended to the delight of all.[21]

Like many other prominent Southerners, then, Page illustrates the divided mind of the postwar South, and he shows it in his person no less than in his fiction. Having grown to manhood in rural surroundings, he lived his adult life in the city. Reared in the South, he established residence north of the Potomac in 1893 and spent most of his remaining thirty years in Washington. Professing a distaste for materialism, he moved in such fashionable circles in the nation's capital that his life style demanded considerable wealth—a requirement met by the resources of his wife, sister-in-law of Marshall Field by a former marriage. Contemptuous of the ill-advised schemes of Reconstruction businessmen, he himself plunged into a chimerical speculative venture in western Virginia mines.[22] These events, contradictory in hindsight, failed to impress Page as such. His mind, divided to us, was one to him, as were the Old South and the New South. "The New South," he emphasized again, "is . . . only the Old South with Slavery gone and the fire of exaction on its back."[23]

To quench the fire, the New South, Page felt, needed power, and power came through progress. He looked approvingly upon material advancement in his native region and worked to effect it. He advocated industrialization, controlled utilization of mineral resources, and an efficient and extensive transportation system. All these things, moreover, would come to pass because a higher power had ordained them.[24] If his judgment of the South's accomplishments since Reconstruction was less sanguine than, say, Grady's, his vision of the region's possibilities was extravagantly optimistic. Appalachian Virginia, for instance, he believed "destined to become one of the most prosperous and wealthy regions in the entire country."[25] He had fallen into the same trap that ensnared those New South promoters who believed that the mere presence of abundant natural resources meant prosperity for the people of the South.

Page failed to see the error in his thinking, and throughout the 1890s his interest in the New South movement increased to such an extent that in 1903 he addressed himself to it in fiction, the medium he formerly reserved for recollections of the past. The Plantation Tradition remained alive, however, even in *Gordon Keith*, a novel rife with nostalgia and sentimentality.

This "salute to the New South" relates the adventures of the title character from his boyhood on the old plantation to success as a businessman of the New South.[26] Gordon is a child when the Civil War breaks out and disrupts the idyllic life at Elphinstone, the family's estate in the Piedmont of Virginia. His father, a hero of the Mexican War, joins the Confederate forces and quickly becomes a general officer. Wounded late in the conflict and forced from duty in the field, General Keith serves briefly as Confederate envoy in England, taking Gordon with him. Upon their return to Elphinstone, the war ends and hard times begin in earnest for the Keiths.

The disruptions of war are as nothing compared with the evils of Reconstruction. Faced with financial ruin, General Keith adamantly refuses refuge in the bankruptcy laws. Elphinstone falls to the auctioneer's hammer and is purchased by Aaron Wickersham, a New York capitalist friendly to the corrupt Reconstruction government of the state. Though General Keith shuns the new proprietor's politics, he remains at Elphinstone to manage the estate for Wickersham.

Now nearing manhood, Gordon takes work with an engineering party surveying lines for a proposed railroad through the mineral-rich mountains to the west of Elphinstone. His willingness to work and his pleasant disposition earn him the goodwill of the Northern supervisor, which in turn rekindles the enmity of Aaron Wickersham's son Ferdy, with whom Gordon had fought as a boy in England. Throughout the remainder of the novel, Page takes pains to contrast Gordon, the gentlemanly Southerner, with young Wickersham, the symbol of the dissolute *nouveau riche*.

While working with the surveyors, Gordon renews the Keith family's friendship with Adam Rawson, a substantial landowner in the western part of the state. Squire Rawson blocks the right-of-way of the proposed railroad and refuses to sell his mineral rights to the Northern development company. He does, however, arrange a loan for Gordon, which is sufficient to get him started in college. Young Keith makes the most of the opportunity, enters college, and after an interruption to work as a mountain teacher, completes his formal education.

Gordon chooses not to return to teaching and instead moves to Gumbolt, a rough mining camp back in the mountains. After facing down the local bully, he establishes himself as a leader and becomes the town marshal. Meanwhile, Squire Rawson, having bought up the mineral rights of other landowners in the area, relents in his opposition to economic development of the region and commissions Gordon, who has shown ability as a mining engineer, to act as his agent in the construction of mines and a railroad.

Finding it necessary to spend much time in New York in search of Northern capital to help effect this development, Gordon is momentarily impressed by the glitter of fashionable society. Success goes to his head as he interests an English syndicate in developing the squire's holdings and in the process earns thousands of dollars for himself. He soon perceives his new arrogance, however, and, guided by his father, repents by using some of the money to help save a Northern friend from financial disaster. He then rejects fashionable society, successfully woos a Northern-born childhood acquaintance, returns to Gumbolt—now renamed appropriately New Leeds—and lives happily ever after.

Throughout the novel, Page disparages the materialistic ethic of the Gilded Age, leading some scholars to read *Gordon Keith* as an attack upon the New South movement.[27] But Page associates crass materialism with the North, first with the fraudulent schemes of Reconstruction and later with the sham world of New York fashion. The businessmen he disdains are all nouveau Northerners who manipulate rather than produce wealth. His treatment of Gordon diverges significantly from his attitude toward these men he stereotypes as robber barons. Keith personifies what his creator would have the New South be. Honorable, courageous, astute, Gordon functions famously in the New Order as he remembers fondly the Old. Though the tinseled world of Northern fashion tempts him briefly, he chooses finally the more substantial Southern way and works for the region's progress from his office in New Leeds.

That Gordon comes back to New Leeds rather than to Elphinstone, which he had purchased earlier, does not symbolize to Page a break with the past.[28] Gordon's return is instead an affirmation of the moral superiority of the South's past and, for that matter, of the present. Whether his return be to New Leeds or to Elphinstone, it is still to the South, ordered, traditional, conscious of its unique identity. It was Page's view of the New South movement as conservative that enabled him to sanction it. Earlier, he had opposed political groups in Virginia that appeared radical and not quite respectable, the Readjusters and the Populists among them. Like other men of the New South persuasion, he refused to acknowledge that the core of their movement, the appeal for industrialization, was a radical departure from the region's past. Instead, he cast that development in a traditional light and made it appear conservative. On one occasion he noted with approval that Virginians had built the first iron foundry in America, so they surely had not objected to industrialism.[29]

Through dialogue, characterization, plot development, and authorial comment, Page makes clear in *Gordon Keith* his attitude toward the New South of material advancement. Even General Keith, the embodiment of the Old South and therefore an admirable character, favors economic development if it is managed by the right people, that is, Southerners or Northerners qua Southerners.[30] Squire Rawson, a sympathetically drawn character, initially opposes the efforts of the Northern company trying to purchase his land and mineral rights. At first we think he resists because he rejects the prospect of a colonial economy for the South. That is not the case, however, for later he sells his holdings, through his agent Keith, to an English syndicate. Neither does the squire refuse to sell because he opposes on principle the changes railroads and mines will bring. His reason is merely that he desires a lion's share of the proceeds for himself. After he learns of the Northern company's plans, he begins secretly to buy up the mineral rights of other landowners without telling them of the development that will increase the value of their holdings.[31] When the Northern company circulates misleading information in an attempt to secure mineral rights at a diminished price, it is duplicity. When Squire Rawson withholds information for the same end, it is good business. There is a strange conscience at work here; the Potomac River affects its judgment.

Page's description of the transformation of Gumbolt into New Leeds also shows his approval of material progress. The railroad that penetrates the mountains causes the little mining village to undergo a metamorphosis "from a chrysalis to a full-fledged butterfly with wings unfolding in the sun of prosperity."[32] Any inclination to believe that Page penned this inappropriate nature metaphor with tongue in cheek is dispelled in ensuing descriptions. Within a year the "straggling village" of Gumbolt becomes "a town . . . beginning to put on the airs of a city."[33] It is permissible, even desirable, for urbanization to come to the South, for surely New Leeds will never sustain an effete society like that Keith has seen in New York. On the contrary, the results of the Southern city's energy and vigor are evident everywhere: "Brick buildings . . . were springing up where a year before there were unsightly frame boxes; the roads where hogs had wallowed in mire . . . were becoming well-paved streets. . . . [Where there] had been a forest, [there] were sprinkled sightly dwellings in pretty yards."[34] Even in a promotional tract distorting the contributions of the New York–based Wickersham enterprises to the area, the truest statement, the author points out, is the account of the rise of New Leeds. And though bust eventually follows boom in the city, that misfortune results from the instability of the Wickersham company, now under the management of Keith's enemy Ferdy.[35]

Not only the business slump in New Leeds but almost every other unfortunate occurrence in the novel can be blamed upon the fashionable society of New York. It causes the dissolution of Keith's first love affair. It sustains the profligate Ferdy Wickersham, who causes only suffering for others. With its belief in money as the mark of a man, it encourages unscrupulous businessmen to get rich at all costs.

Page employs the Plantation Tradition in an attempt to expose the shallowness of urban society by contrasting it with the Old Order. But city life has its attractions for Keith as it did for Page himself. Moreover, the author sentimentalizes the Old Order to such an extent that he cannot make it live. The Old South is a dream world peopled by ghosts. Though the novel is filled with stereotyped characters, no other is as lifeless as General Keith, the symbol of the Old Order.

If Page cannot substitute the dream of the Old South for the reality of the postwar North, he does the next best thing. He carries as much as he can of the Old into the New South and lets that world stand as an alternative to the grasping North. To Page, the South is a progressive yet conservative society that rejects materialism. The North produces Ferdy Wickershams; the South, Gordon Keiths. As the author tells us in the first sentence of the novel, Keith is a gentleman. But he is also an enthusiastic apostle of the gospel of work, and, as Page makes clear, a gentleman can also be a capitalist. Keith, then, is the Old South and the New made one. For him, as for many flesh-and-blood Southerners, progress is "a new charge at Gettysburg, which should finally and incontestably win for [the South] the right to be itself, for which . . . it had always fought."[36]

In *Gordon Keith*, Page decrees that the South will indeed have progress, but on its own terms. Its quest for riches will in no way diminish its moral superiority. The aristocratic impulse will remain strong. The best people—that is, the well-born—will control the South's destiny. The other whites, to whom Page helplessly condescends, will be satisfied with their inferior station. And the black man—there is not a single Negro character in *Gordon Keith*—will become but a cipher. Of progress there will be an abundance, but of social mobility a minimum. The New South will thrive and sustain the Old.

If the body of Page's writing put him at the front of plantation romancers, no other single work established the Plantation Tradition more firmly in the popular mind than F. Hopkinson Smith's

Colonel Carter of Cartersville.[37] Appearing at the height of the New South movement, this short novel, like Page's works, celebrates the memory of the Old South as it endorses the New Order.

Like his friend Page, Smith was a native Southerner of an old and respected family. Born in 1838 in a genteel area of Baltimore, he numbered among his ancestors Francis Hopkinson, early American poet and signer of the Declaration of Independence. With long-standing Virginia connections, Smith's family enjoyed in Baltimore a life style similar to that of the well-born across the Chesapeake Bay. The great house "with the old darkies polishing . . . and washing . . . in the early morning lingered in his memory." But harsher memories remained too. As young Smith prepared for college, reversals in the family's fortunes forced him to give up that prospect and go to work. First in a hardware store and then in an iron foundry, he entered the world of trade and industry.[38]

When war broke out in 1861, Smith apparently felt little compulsion to join the Confederate army, for he moved to New York to work again in a foundry. He soon left that occupation, however, to become a civil engineer. His career in that field was one of considerable achievement, especially in the construction of marine projects such as lighthouses, seawalls, and the foundation for the Statue of Liberty.[39]

Once established as an engineer, Smith gave his leisure hours to painting. His interest and his talent were of such a degree that painting soon became more than just a hobby. He began to illustrate books by others and then to make sketches for the travel books he himself wrote.[40]

The composition of travel accounts led Smith into a third career, authorship. Among the clubmen of New York he already enjoyed a reputation as an entertaining teller of stories of the old plantation. At the urging of Richard Watson Gilder of *Century Magazine*, he committed these tales to paper, incorporating them into *Colonel Carter of Cartersville*, a novel published serially in 1890 in the *Century* and the following year in book form.[41] Past fifty when he wrote *Colonel Carter*, Smith devoted much of the rest of his life to writing, though infrequently to treatment of Southern topics.[42] It is ironic that this man who left the South, loved the metropolis, never lived in a rural environment, and who, like Page, was a cosmopolitan socialite, should have his literary reputation rest upon his evocation of the Old South through the Plantation Tradition.

Set in the early 1880s, *Colonel Carter* opens with the protagonist, George Fairfax Carter, former officer in the Confederate army and master of Carter Hall, the ancestral estate near the hamlet of Cartersville, Virginia, away from home, living temporarily in New York. He has come to the city to promote the Cartersville and Warrentown Air Line Railroad, a project existing only in his mind but one he is confident will bring riches to himself and to Virginia. His Northern friends humor him, though they entertain little hope for the success of his venture. Nevertheless, through the efforts of Mr. Fitzpatrick, Carter's friend and a leading Wall Street financier, an English syndicate takes an interest in the colonel's property— the "Garden Spot of Virginia"—not for the purposes of railroad construction but for the possibility of exploiting the property's coal deposits.

At this point the scene changes from New York to Carter Hall. The colonel, his Northern friends, and the representative of the English investors journey to Virginia to determine whether the coal is indeed on Carter's land. They discover the object of their search to be part of the Carter estate but the property of the colonel's Aunt Nancy, not his own. Aunt Nancy, of course, wants what is best for George and relinquishes title to the coal land. The colonel then sells it to the English syndicate, receives a handsome price, and prepares to restore the remainder of the Carter estate to its former grandeur.

Many standard elements of the Plantation Tradition appear in the novel, the central one being Colonel Carter himself. His very appearance suggests nobility. Tall, slender, military in bearing, Carter has iron-gray hair of collar length, deep-set eyes, prominent nose, high brow, firm mouth, strong jaw, and gray mustache and goatee. His voice, soft and low, is "tempered with a cadence that is delicious." He is proper yet unreserved, frank yet tactful, proud yet unpretentious. Though the world has treated him harshly since the war, he remains good-humored and optimistic.[43]

Other characters also fit snugly into the tradition. Never has there been a more loyal servant than Carter's man Chad. He exists solely to serve the colonel. Only two developments detract from Chad's happiness: the temporary residence in New York away from the old plantation and the Thirteenth Amendment to the Constitution. For though he is content to serve from custom, he would prefer to remain a chattel. Like Page's Sam in "Marse

Chan," Chad, the black man, affirms more strongly than anyone else the glory of the Old Order. As he tells the narrator, one of the colonel's Northern friends, "Dem was high times. We ain't neber seed no time like dat since de war."[44] Only Chad's return to Carter Hall can bring back a measure of the happiness he enjoyed thirty years before.

Smith reaches the apogee of the Plantation Tradition in his description of the Southern lady. Delicate, refined, seldom intimate, yet always cordial, the colonel's Aunt Nancy, though aged, retains a hint of the fragile beauty that marked her youth—a "bit of old porcelain," the colonel calls her.[45] The other characters, especially Carter, worship her and fix her so high on the pedestal of adulation that she could never descend even if she desired. And of course she does not, for she knows that that is her proper place. She is a kind of goddess who floats—Smith never lets her walk—through a dream world evocative of the Old Order.

It is as a dream world, a never-never land, that the Old South impresses us, though ostensibly Smith was trying to make it real for postwar readers. Chad's recollections of antebellum days at Carter Hall picture life there as an unending succession of feasting and dancing and courting. But what supported this grand style? It is impossible to tell. No one, it seems, ever worked. The house servants frolicked just as the whites did, and the field hands— presumably they were legion, and happy, too—never appear in Chad's recollections. Affairs must have run smoothly and of their own accord, however, for General John Carter, the colonel's father, never concerned himself with business matters.[46] But this, after all, was as it should have been. To Smith the Southern planter was anything but a businessman, and the plantation, for all its ease and picturesqueness, was merely a nice place to visit, which is what the narrator, who stands for Smith, does.

Because Smith believed what he wrote of the Old South, that society did not provide for him an alternative to contemporary America. On the contrary, New York circa 1890 was good enough for this man of the world whom success greeted on each new endeavor. Despite his sympathy for Colonel Carter as a symbol of the plantation regime, Smith gives ample evidence that he cannot quite take the colonel, or certain aspects of the Old Order, seriously.

Through his treatment of the code duello, he even satirizes, albeit good-naturedly, the Old South's proudest possession, its conception of honor. The colonel feels he has been offended by one P. A. Klutchem, a stockbroker who jests crudely about Carter's railroad scheme. What follows is a comedy of errors. Carter issues a challenge by mail, fails to stamp the letter, brands Klutchem a coward for not responding, yields finally to the arguments of Fitzpatrick that the affront is only imagined, insists upon apologizing publicly to Klutchem, and denounces him roundly when denied that opportunity.[47]

The duel sequence, moreover, allows Smith to bring in two other Southern characters, Judge I. B. Kerfoot and Major Tom Yancey, friends of the colonel who come to New York to act as seconds in the encounter with Klutchem. To Carter his houseguests are models, respectively, of legal acumen and military skill. To Fitzpatrick, however, they are "fire-eaters," and to Smith they are fit subjects for satire. Provincial, penniless, and lazy, they do little but eat, sleep, drink juleps, and order Chad about.[48]

Smith's satirization of the South's exaggerated sense of honor reaches a high point in Carter's story of Colonel Temple Talcott. Friend to Carter and Virginia gentleman of the old school, Talcott twice requests of a Yankee postmaster the loan of a three-cent stamp. When the scoundrel refuses, Talcott draws his revolver and shoots him, the only recourse open to a man of honor, Carter feels.[49]

Admirable though Carter is in many ways—we might even concede him his strange sense of honor—he is often little more than a buffoon. Though his Northern friends point out that his proposed railway is only a branch road with no trunk line within miles, the colonel feels this to be an advantage because there will be no competition.[50] He fails also to appreciate the worth of the coal deposits on the Carter estate. His lack of political sophistication rivals his ignorance of business matters. As the narrator explains, Carter "chafes continually under what he believes to be the tyranny . . . of an undefined autocracy, which in a general way, he calls 'the Government,' but which really refers to the distribution of certain local offices in his own immediate vicinity."[51] Refusing to pay taxes on the tobacco produced at Carter Hall, the colonel accuses the government of robbing Southerners of their substance. On "cross-examination [he] could not locate any particular wholesale robbery, but it did not check the flow of his indignation."[52] Not only does he know little of economics in the large, he cannot even handle his personal financial affairs. Seldom does he know how much money is in his pockets, which, Smith implies, is just as well, because they are usually empty. Carter believes the passbook arrangement for buying food is designed merely as a courtesy to him and gives no thought to paying his bill. When his friend Fitzpatrick reminds him that the rent on his office is due, the colonel replies that he will not insult his landlords by lowering his relationship with them to the level of dollars and cents.[53] The comedy in such episodes derives, as in *Huckleberry Finn*, from the reader's knowledge and the protagonist's ignorance of the humor of the situation. But though there is nothing extraordinary in such treatment of an unlettered urchin from backwoods Missouri, one hardly expects a Virginia gentleman to be so patronized.

One Southern critic caught the drift of what Smith had done to Carter and objected. John S. Patton protested that "that amiable character is not, in strictness, a gentleman of the old school in the South. In the South as elsewhere, it is not the gentleman who is a type of the best life who borrows money and habitually forgets to repay it."[54] As if Smith anticipated such criticism, he makes sure that Carter's naiveté prevails in the sophisticated world of business. The colonel is the proverbial country boy, notwithstanding his eminent social position, who endures the vicissitudes of urban life and triumphs in the end. Even though he is unaccustomed to the workings of Wall Street, his endorsement of a stock hastily raises its value, for his enthusiasm is contagious and can boom any property. His grace and hospitality to the grocer dissuade that worthy from collecting the colonel's account, though Carter is of course unconscious of what he is doing.[55] Although he knows nothing of business matters, with the help of Providence and Aunt Nancy, he winds up a rich man. The Old South, then, for which Carter is the symbol, can function in the New Order, but significantly it does so by accident rather than by design.

In keeping with the Plantation Tradition, the myth of the Old South in *Colonel Carter* not only survives but grows stronger in the New South. To Smith, as to other New South spokesmen, a major result of the new dispensation would be to restore through business the eminence the Old Order had achieved through politics.[56] Even the colonel can see this. "Think," he advises his Northern friends, "of the effect that a colossal financial concern like the great

British syndicate would produce upon Fairfax County."[57] Though part and parcel of the Old South, he has no quarrel with the New.

Smith also believed the two could get along well. The novel's final scene shows this conclusively. After the colonel receives the first installment on the coal land, he is a rich man, successful by the standards of the New South. Yet his new wealth fails to turn his head. He thinks instead of the repairs he will make on Carter Hall. He assures Chad that the rest of his days will consist only of un-interrupted leisure. And, as the novel closes, he toasts "that greatest of all blessings,—a true Southern lady [Aunt Nancy]!"[58] Smith has placed the Plantation Tradition—model mansion, idyllic race relations, and idealized Southern womanhood—in the New South, to the delight of all.

Above all else, the Old South as created by Smith and by Page was picturesque, even in its faults. Paradoxically, these writers, who wanted intensely to keep the past alive, killed it, for as Allen Tate has remarked, "the moment the past becomes picturesque it is dead."[59] But even though dead in its own right, the Southern past still had its uses, not the least of which was the reinforcement of the New South movement.

IV.

PIEDMONT UTOPIA:
THOMAS DIXON, JR., AND
WILL N. HARBEN

Rivaling the popularity of Page and Smith was the work of a younger contemporary, Thomas Dixon, Jr. All three agreed that the South's brave new age had arrived; the major difference in their thought was their attitude toward the Negro. Dixon's work lacks the paternalistic view of the black man conspicuous in the writing of Page and Smith. The contrasting perceptions of the Negro were largely the product of each writer's formative environment.

Born in 1864 near Shelby, North Carolina, the son of a Baptist preacher, Dixon grew up in an area that was a hotbed of Ku Klux-ism. Not of the gentry, he was self-made and worked at many occupations during his long life: the ministry, the law, politics, acting, lecturing, writing. Remembered primarily for his virulently racist views, he disseminated his negrophobia through fiction and through the motion picture *Birth of a Nation*, made from his novel *The Clansman*. Of the twenty-two novels he wrote, three dealing directly with Reconstruction are pertinent here. Unconcerned with creating a story for its own sake, Dixon used fiction, as he himself admitted, to write what he, at least, contended was history.[1] In the Reconstruction trilogy, the history is fictitious indeed.

Dixon's interpretation of Southern history was distorted by his racism, a topic dealt with at length elsewhere.[2] But there is also in the Reconstruction trilogy a recurring auxiliary theme directly related to the New South movement. Through all three novels Dixon comments upon the economic changes occurring after the Civil War.

In a perceptive piece on Dixon, F. Garvin Davenport, Jr., has pointed out a connection between the major theme of the trilogy, the Negro, and the secondary theme of economic change. In the black man's new role as citizen, he stood as the symbol of all the evils that befell the South during Reconstruction. To Dixon this hideous creation was the work of a Northern urban-industrial environment that, having fashioned its monster, made sure it remained below the Potomac.[3] Fortunately for civilization, the fiercely independent, racially pure, Anglo-Saxon South would have none of this and, following the dictates of a law higher than man's, restored the white race to its natural place of dominance.

By eliminating the debilitative influence of black men in Southern society, Dixon's racial policy, which included proposals to deport Negroes, would insure, he believed, a strong South. So, too, would his ideas for the New South's economy. If, as Davenport maintains, there was in Dixon a longing for the lost world of the plantation society, that feeling was as feebly romantic as that in Page's export literature of the Lost Cause.[4] For in the Reconstruction trilogy, Dixon welcomed the industrialization of the South as long as it was controlled by Southerners, an attitude akin to Page's in *Gordon Keith*.

In *The Leopard's Spots*, the first of the Reconstruction novels, a conspicuous and sympathetically drawn character, General Daniel Worth, voices Dixon's belief that manufacturing will help save the South. Like a host of nonfictional Confederate generals, Worth—of course, he had opposed secession—carries the standard of the New South movement. His textile mills on the banks of the Catawba in western North Carolina give work to 2,000 people and provide a market, it seems, for all the South's cotton. This miraculous development, Worth maintains, is the result of faith and waterpower.

Waterpower ranks second only to the general's daughter Sallie as his favorite topic of conversation. As he says on two separate occasions, "we've got water-power enough [in the South] to turn every wheel in the world." To Worth the sound of turning wheels is "ravishing music." The machinery in his mills he imagines to be "a living thing, with millions of fingers of steel and a great throbbing soul." Soon "those mighty fingers will weave their fabrics of gold and clothe the whole South in splendour." In that great day, says Worth, the South will have become "what God meant her to be, the garden of the world."[5] And, he might have added, supply merchant to the human race.

According to Dixon, General Worth is the kind of forward-looking leader the South needs. Throughout the novels of Reconstruction, vision and wisdom are peculiarly Southern traits, even if possessed by a character such as Phil Stoneman. Though a native Northerner and a Union veteran, young Stoneman, a leading character in *The Clansman*, is a naturalized Southerner. Notwithstanding his father's resemblance to Thaddeus Stevens, Phil helps the South Carolina upcountrymen resist Radical Republicanism, courts a Southern maiden in finest chivalric fashion, and voices the proper views concerning the Negro and the South's economic development. Out of military defeat, Stoneman says, will come the South's salvation, for the region "will yet rise to a nobler life than [it] . . . ever lived in the past." Manufacturing will play a major part in the South's triumphant future, and Stoneman, a man of "genius, skill, and enterprise," leads the movement for industrial development by organizing a textile company.[6]

To effect this economic regeneration through industrialization both Stoneman and Worth have the help of Northern capital. Even so, their mills are Southern enterprises, a fact Dixon reinforces in *The Traitor*, the last of the Reconstruction novels. As that story ends, John Graham, former leader of North Carolina's Ku Klux Klan, has organized a cotton mill with local capital and made a Northern man its superintendent. But Ackerman, the superintendent, is safe, for he has married a Southern woman and by the current fictional formula has become a Southerner himself. One feels, moreover, that the mill is much more a philanthropic venture than a business designed to earn profits for the owner.[7]

Like the postbellum plantation romancers, Dixon would eat his cake and still have it. That is, like Page and Smith, he created a South triumphant in the world of business and yet innocent of the crass materialism prevalent in the philistine North. In Dixon's fiction, the New South nurtures the mythic ideals of the Old. "No dollar mark has yet been placed on the doors of Southern society," says Charles Gaston, the protagonist of *The Leopard's Spots*. The Reverend Mr. John Durham tells a Bostonian, "you prosperous Yankees can't get into your heads the idea that there are many things which money can't measure." The South, Durham adds, stands against urban corruption and all the other evils of "undigested wealth" common to the North. General Worth's mills sit not in some ugly city but beside his plantation mansion, an image fittingly reflecting Dixon's ideas. Worth's factories, moreover, produce music, not the discordant roar of machinery as in, say, Lowell, Massachusetts.[8] Dixon fits snugly into the mold of New South spokesmen piercingly cracked by John Donald Wade when he wrote of their movement: "Its program was, while speaking reverently, always of the past, to repudiate that past as rapidly as ever one might—with one exception, that the nigger be kept to his place."[9]

In Dixon's Reconstruction novels the black man is bound securely in his place. No Negro will find work in the mills of Daniel Worth, Phil Stoneman, and John Graham. No Negro will venture to vote after Charles Gaston becomes governor of North Carolina. No Negro will presume to run for office once the Klan has purged the South of Radicalism. When the black man is reduced to a cipher or, better, banished from the land, and when an industrial economy comes to the South, then all right-thinking white men will live happily ever after.

The protagonists of Dixon's Reconstruction novels—Charles Gaston, Ben Cameron, and John Graham—are classic Southern gentlemen fallen on hard times. This is true also of the protagonists in much other postbellum fiction, who achieve material success in the New South not through planting but by casting their lot with the new industrial economy. As many of them profess fidelity to the Cavalier ideal with its renunciation of materialism, they reject, as Ben Cameron, the protagonist of *The Clansman*, says, the "idea that Southern boys are lazy, loafing dreamers."[10] These characters extol the work ethic, and, however much they may demur, they imitate the rising businessman of the North. They seek recognition according to the standards of their time.

Like these fictional characters, some members of the gentry adapted to postbellum conditions and joined in the New South movement. But just as often, according to W. J. Cash, "they neither could nor would meet the demands of the times." If they were forced finally to adjust, they did so "by iotas and jots—fell back by inches. They compromised no more than was required if they were to avoid extinction."[11] Moreover, as Paul M. Gaston has shown, the intellectual leaders of the New South movement were usually men not of planter antecedents but of middle-class and nonrural backgrounds.[12] Theirs was a New South for new men. In this regard the fiction of Will N. Harben mirrors more accurately the actuality of the postwar South.

Born in Dalton, Georgia, in 1858, William Nathaniel Harben spent his first thirty years in North Georgia and East Tennessee.

During his young manhood, he worked unsuccessfully as a merchant.[13] His affairs stayed in arrears because, his wife said later, "He spent all spare time reading and talking, writing his impressions of people who came into his store, paying slight attention to business."[14]

In 1888, Harben left his mountain store and moved to New York, resolved to practice the writer's craft. During the next decade he produced some slight works including detective fiction, a fantastic novel of a suboceanic society, and a story of literary life in New York.[15] But near the end of the century, absence from his native land having made memories of it more poignant, Harben began writing stories set in the hills of North Georgia.[16]

Although *Northern Georgia Sketches*, the collection of these stories, contains little of direct pertinence to social conditions in the postbellum South, Harben occasionally punctures the canvas of the plantation romancers. He portrays slavery, for example, as something other than a benevolent institution and pictures some Confederate soldiers as unheroic.

Northern Georgia Sketches brought Harben recognition as a writer of local-color stories even as that genre was becoming unfashionable. After having composed these stories, he turned his efforts to writing novels and until his death in 1919 produced them at a rate of one a year. William Dean Howells praised Harben for his realistic portrayal of a little-known region and people, a judgment echoed by scholars.[17] Although there are limits to his realism, a recent critic has observed that Harben handles competently his "sociological theme . . . [of] the ascendant middle-class ideal in the New South."[18]

One novel, among many others that deal tangentially with the issues raised by the New South movement, treats directly the theme of economic progress. Published in 1902 and set near the town of Darley, which is based on Dalton, *Abner Daniel* tells the story of the Bishop family, middle-class Georgians of the 1890s who profit greatly from the coming of the railroad. Alfred Bishop, the head of the family, owns a fair-sized farm and speculates in timberlands. Tricked into thinking a railroad is to be constructed near Darley, Bishop increases his holdings of woodlands by buying 5,000 acres, selling some valuable cotton-mill stocks and mortgaging his farm to make the purchase. Shortly thereafter, he learns the truth and, land-poor, despairs of ever becoming wealthy.

But his son Alan, the protagonist of the story, forms a plan to save the family. Enlisting the help of Rayburn Miller, a shrewd lawyer and speculator, Alan proposes to build a branch road from the nearest trunk line to the great timberlands near Darley. Miller interests the Southern Land and Timber Company of Atlanta in Alan's proposition, through its agent Wilson, a native Bostonian. Wilson lends $25,000 to the Bishops, hoping to foreclose later and take their largest single tract for much less than its value. By an elaborate ruse, Miller convinces Wilson that the Bishops can get the money elsewhere to pay off the note and no longer need his help. Wilson then agrees to buy the tract for $100,000, quadrupling old Bishop's investment, and to have the timber company finance construction of the railroad if the other mountain farmers will grant free right-of-way. Alan and Miller, with the aid of Alan's uncle, Abner Daniel, persuade the reluctant farmers to reap the benefits of progress the road will bring. All ends happily as Alan, now a rich man, plans to marry the wealthy Dolly Barclay; Miller wins the hand of Alan's sister Adele; and the whole region joyously anticipates the blessings of prosperity.

Although Abner Daniel is not the protagonist of the story, Harben uses him more than any other character to comment upon the social and economic issues raised in the novel. A sixty-year-old bachelor, Daniel is a crossroads philosopher, a skeptic in religious matters, and an ardent advocate of economic progress. How the South achieves material success matters not to him. He condones, even relishes, the less than straightforward tactics of Ray Miller, reasoning, along with Alan Bishop, that Miller deals with shifty men and must therefore be guileful himself.

Daniel echoes his creator, for Harben shows in many episodes his admiration for the speculators and traders of the New South. Landowners, timber buyers, and railroad agents delight in opportunities to deceive one another. Though seemingly foolish at first, Alfred Bishop's speculative ventures finally turn an enormous profit. Ray Miller is the shrewdest speculator of all, a man rich at thirty-three from the many deals he has manipulated.[19]

Harben handles many of the trading sequences humorously, after the fashion of another Georgian, Augustus Baldwin Longstreet, the author of *Georgia Scenes*. But Ray Miller plays for much higher stakes than Peter Ketch.[20] The trades in *Abner Daniel* are not the horse swaps of the Old Southwest but the large business transactions of the New South. Because of the gravity of the situations, the humor appears inappropriate. It does, however, enable Harben, through characters such as Alan Bishop, Miller, and Daniel, to excuse the prevailing business ethic of dog-eat-dog. If one can laugh at the traders, then their actions seem less blameworthy.

Abner Daniel is particularly satisfied with Miller's triumph over Wilson in the Bishop land deal. It gratifies his sectional pride to see the smug Yankee brought down from his lofty perch. Acting as a slow-witted, lazy, unsophisticated country lawyer, Miller deceives Wilson easily. He does this so adroitly that the obtuse Northerner fails to perceive what has happened, calling Miller a "drowsy Southerner . . . [who] will [never] get over [his] habit of sleeping during business hours."[21] Notwithstanding the duplicity of both Miller and Wilson, no harm is done. The Bishops fare well, Wilson's company will make money, and progress will come to North Georgia.

The symbol of this progress, achieved by whatever means, is the railroad, which is, moreover, an exclusively Southern enterprise. The men who plan it are Georgians; a Southerner outwits a Northerner to effect its construction; the company that finances it is Georgian. There is no hint of outside control. At a time when railroad lines were falling into the colonial pattern of much of the rest of the Southern economy, this was manifestly an unrealistic touch.

To convince the conservative farmers that granting the railroad free right-of-way is the wise course, the right-thinking characters organize a meeting at Springtown, a village near Darley. As agent of the company to finance construction, Wilson tactlessly advises the farmers that if they will be considered intelligent men they must approve the railroad, which will "dispel darkness where it had reigned since the dawn of civilization."[22]

Miller rises to try and repair the damage done by Wilson. He assures the gathering that if Wilson's oratory is poor his intentions are good. Pointing out that Springtown is the native ground of the Miller family, the lawyer asserts that he wants only good fortune for the area. Inappropriately linking the steam engine to benign nature, he says, "I want to see [Springtown] bloom in progress and blossom like the rose of prosperity." Then, he resorts to extravagant descriptions of the South's resources common among promoters. The mineral wealth of the Georgia mountains is so vast, he maintains, that it can "benefit . . . mankind wherever God's sunlight falls."[23]

Still unpersuaded that the projected railroad is the godsend it is purported to be, the farmers are ready to reject the promoters' request for free right-of-way. At this point, however, Abner Daniel takes the platform to strike a blow for progress. Through folksy anecdotes he puts the audience at ease and at the same time chides it for the region's backwardness. He relates his exchange, probably apocryphal, with a railroad flagman in Darley who branded the people of Short Pine District around Springtown "mossbacks" that "don't know the war's over; a nigger from over thar come in town t'other day an' heard fer the fust time that he was free. Two men over thar swapped wives without knowin' thar was a law agin it. Half o' you-uns never laid eyes on a railroad, an' wouldn't have one as a free gift."[24]

Abner admits that though these barbs stung him, they were as nothing compared with the remarks of a peddler selling maps of the United States. Wanting to buy a map, Abner tells the gathering, he wished to examine one first. Upon looking at the map, he found Short Pine District covered with dots. He learned from the peddler that the dots "indicate the amount o' ignorance in a locality." Moreover, the drummer tells Daniel, "You'll find 'em in all places away from the railroads; a body kin say what they please agin railroads, but they fetch schools, an' books, an' enlightenment." Abner agrees that the only thing to push the dots off the map is the cowcatcher of a steam engine.[25]

What Harben failed to have the peddler say was that railroads also brought the virtual monopoly of J. Pierpont Morgan with its Northern control of the Southern systems, unfavorable freight-rate differentials, and the absorption of millions of acres of Southern land by rail companies.[26] Unwittingly, though, Harben argues for the farmers forcefully and accurately. Joe Bartell, the leader of the opposition, describes the nature of the South's exploitation by railroads and extractive industries. He knows that the projected line will benefit the promoters greatly, but he asks the other farmers, "what have *we* got to do with this trade? Nothin' as I kin see. But we are expected to yell an' holler, an' deed [the promoters] a free right of way through our property so they kin ship the timber straight through to the North an' turn it into cold Yankee coin. We don't count in this shuffle."[27]

Bartell's position is not, however, Harben's. An unsympathetically drawn character, Bartell is a political opportunist who abandons his stand in exchange for the promise of votes. Moreover, as
Miller says earlier of Bartell's attitude, "it's tough on human progress."[28]

To Harben a progressive society is one of self-made individuals.
Almost every admirable character in his novels fits into this cate-
gory: the Bishops and Ray Miller, Nelson Floyd, Ann Boyd and
Luke King, Gilbert Neal, Dixie Hart, and Alfred Henley.[29] These
people move up in the world by hard work, thrift, a willingness to
speculate, and a disregard for tradition. Luke King, a mountain boy
become Atlanta editor, is proud to have come from "the new . . .
log-cabin aristocracy."[30] Another character describes him as a man
unawed by the old gentry, a man whose "clear eye doesn't waver
as he stares steadily into the face [of an aristocrat] as if to see if the
old regime has left a fragment of brains there worth respecting."[31]

To King, and to Harben, many remnants of the Old Order are
shabby indeed. Langdon Chester, a scion of the gentry and King's
rival for a maiden's hand, drinks excessively, gambles regularly,
uses women, insults so-called social inferiors, and considers work
an abomination designed only for the lower orders. Chester Sively,
Langdon's cousin and a decent enough fellow, could not compete
under the new dispensation were it not for an inheritance.[32] The
late Ben Warren, "a delicate flower," wallowed in affectation, en-
forced inane rules on his plantation, furnished his mansion taste-
lessly, and had breakfast in bed every morning.[33] Alfred Henley, a
sturdy merchant, thinks such a life style "a joke."[34]

And yet, though Harben casts away the husks of tradition, he
holds back and uses what he considers the healthy growths. His
New South is an ideal place. As depicted in *The Georgians*, Darley
is a thriving town with a new cotton mill. "But this material progress and awakening of financial interests," Harben maintains, "had
done little towards altering the hearts and manners of the inhabitants." The men are chivalrous as of old, and everyone is delight-
fully polite. Descendants of the aristocracy stand behind store
counters "as gracefully as their forebears had presided at State
dinners or danced at country balls." A South Carolinian regrets
that his state clings too tightly to custom as Georgia forges ahead
commercially while she takes second place to no state in social
standing.[35]

But the gracious shopkeepers of Darley whom Harben admires fix tacks in window ledges to keep idlers from sitting and whittling as in earlier times. For quaint though these men be, they disrupt trade and give the town an appearance of leisure ill-suited to its new image. The new men of the New South—and even if they are of gentry stock, they are self-made—will not tolerate indolence. Ambitious men, they always want more, even when, like Ray Miller and Alfred Henley, they are already well off. And though they own land, they themselves cease to farm it, preferring instead to move to town and seek their fortunes in business. Harben is proud to relate that, to a man, they succeed.

For all his too-uncritical treatment of the self-made men and his too-sanguine estimate of the results of progress, Harben was a keener observer of Southern society than his contemporary, Dixon. Here and there in the Georgian's novels one finds reservations about the New Order. The textile industry employs weak women and children instead of the able-bodied men.[36] Mine owners pay workers too little for a dangerous and difficult job.[37] Business ethics could stand improvement.[38]

Nevertheless, Harben shared the false optimism common to the New South. Carlton Blathwait, a sympathetically portrayed industrial promoter in *The Georgians*, tells another character that the "whole South is looking up." Speaking of Darley, Blathwait continues, "One of these days this little mountain town . . ."[39] Just then the conversation is interrupted, but knowing Harben's sympathies and style one might conjecture he would have concluded Blathwait's remarks in this fashion: . . . will blossom forth in prosperity as the rhododendrons bloom in springtime. History proved Harben wrong. The little mountain town sits on the fringe of one of the most poverty-ridden areas in America, Appalachia, a citadel of want and a symbol of the failure of natural resources, exploitative capital, and village entrepreneurs to generate prosperity.

PART III

THE ILLS OF THE SOUTH:
LITERARY OPPONENTS OF
THE NEW SOUTH MOVEMENT

V.

ANOTHER NEW SOUTH: SIDNEY LANIER AND THE MENACE OF TRADE

Whether memorialists of the old regime or champions of the bourgeoisie, the literary proponents of the New South movement could not distance themselves far enough from the prevailing postbellum ideology to focus upon its flaws. Optimistic over the South's future under the new dispensation, these writers spurned the skepticism that characterized much of the work of some of their contemporaries. Yet before Page and Smith had published anything significant and while Dixon and Harben were still boys, one Southern writer was showing hostility to the New Order.

A sensitive, even sentimental, man, Sidney Lanier was nevertheless a fighter, engaging in many battles during his short life. Not only did he fight Union soldiers, poverty, and tuberculosis, he also contended with trade, the longest and hardest encounter of all. Granting the necessity of getting and spending, of buying and selling, he feared the trade that meant much more than the workings of a small market economy. Leading inevitably to industrialization, big business, and materialism, trade, to Lanier, incorporated all that was unnatural, dehumanizing, and unchristian. He spent much of his life trying to nullify its influence.

Born in Macon, Georgia, in 1842, the son of a lawyer of Huguenot antecedents, Lanier grew up in a middle-class environment. As a boy he learned to play the flute and developed a love for music that subsequently affected his poetic style. His family had means enough to send him to private academies and to Oglethorpe College, where he excelled. Upon graduation from Oglethorpe in 1860, he served as a tutor there for a year, hoping to follow the example of his favorite teacher, James Woodrow, and study later in Germany.[1]

The Civil War crushed that hope. In June 1861, Lanier enlisted eagerly in the Macon Volunteers and proceeded to Virginia. He saw action as a scout for Confederate forces until the fall of 1864 when orders transferred him to duty as a signalman on a blockade runner. En route to that assignment, he was captured at sea and later imprisoned at Point Lookout, Maryland. There he contracted the tuberculosis that would torment him for the rest of his days.[2]

Released from prison and back home in Macon by March 1865, Lanier found that suffering was still his portion. In May of that year his mother died. Straitened circumstances forced the rest of his family to take room and board for a short time at a women's seminary in Macon. To provide, Lanier worked as a tutor and as a hotel clerk in Georgia and Alabama. By the end of 1868 he had returned to Macon to read law in his father's office in search of a way to support his new wife and growing family. For three years he tried his hand at the law but found it dull and unrewarding.[3]

Throughout the difficult postwar years when, as Lanier wrote Bayard Taylor, "pretty much the whole of life has been merely not-dying," his passion for literature grew stronger.[4] Even during the war he had found time to write a few verses and to begin a novel. Although his inability to devote more time to writing disheartened him, he continued to work on the novel after the war and published it as *Tiger-Lilies* in 1867. A poor and often obscure work set in antebellum Tennessee and wartime Virginia, *Tiger-Lilies* tells us little about Lanier's attitude toward the postbellum South. It is instructive, however, as a document in the history of his war on trade, for the antagonist of the story, a product of materialism, is uncomfortable in the presence of nature and music, the higher things in the author's system of values.[5]

In Lanier's early literary efforts, the novel seemed to appeal to him more than the poem as a working form. In 1868, having completed *Tiger-Lilies*, he began working on another novel, but probably because of the need to earn a living he had to put it aside after having written only forty pages.[6] Had he finished "John Lockwood's Mill," it would almost certainly have been one of the earliest novels dealing explicitly with themes of the New South movement. Nevertheless, as the fragment stands, it gives us some idea of what the author was about.

Written while Lanier was teaching in Prattville, Alabama, "John Lockwood's Mill" is set along the Gulf Coast of that state immediately after the Civil War.[7] The plot revolves around the plans of John Lockwood to develop the area of southern Alabama where he

Progress there was in other areas, however, and in some ways Harris welcomed it. But the advancement he admired was not the kind that resulted from industrialization. The industrial impulse spreading like wildfire over much of the South failed to ignite the spark of his imagination. Seldom did his fiction deal with that aspect of Southern life. The progress that appealed to him was of the agrarian variety.

"Aunt Fountain's Prisoner," a story published in 1887, illustrates Harris's views well.[32] The narrator, who speaks for the author, has returned after an extended absence to Rockville in Middle Georgia. He notes "the vast changes that had taken place [since the war]— the most of them for the better. There were new faces and new enterprises . . . and there was a bustle about the town."[33] Yet the new enterprise described in the story is not an industrial, or even a mercantile, establishment. It is rather an agricultural venture, a dairy farm. The new face is that of Ferris Trunion, a former Union soldier wounded in battle who stays on the Tomlinson place after being nursed by the young lady of the house, marries her, and turns old Tomlinson's ruined acres into productive ones. Hard-working, practical, intelligent, Trunion stops Tomlinson's practice of rooting out Bermuda grass. Instead he cultivates it, producing the best pastures and the sleekest cattle in the area. The message here is clear. Change, even if it comes by way of the North, may have beneficent results. But progress in this setting is pastoral; nowhere do we hear the roar of factories.

In "The Old Bascom Place," published four years later and similar in many ways to "Aunt Fountain's Prisoner," Harris shows again his approval of change within a traditional context. Judge Briscoe Bascom, an old planter ruined by the war, returns in the midseventies to the place he formerly owned in Middle Georgia. Embittered, he laments a world in which it is impossible to make money and remain a gentleman. But the author subsequently introduces Francis Underwood and proves Judge Bascom mistaken. The new owner of the old Bascom place and a native Northerner like Ferris Trunion, Underwood, a compassionate man, honors the dying judge's illusion that the place somehow has become his again. Gentleman though Underwood is, he also makes money. Energetic and thrifty, he has made many improvements in Bascom's old place. He raises cattle, breeds horses, grows crops, and operates a sawmill and a cotton gin.[34] He is, in short, an example other farmers might well emulate.

As with Lanier, the New South that gains Harris's favor is a land of productive farms such as Trunion's and Underwood's. Beside them, the "pushing city" of Atlanta with its "dubious ways" appears degenerate indeed.[35] It is as though only the clean air of the country can purify progress and fit it into the Southern agrarian tradition.

To many of Harris's contemporaries, however, progress meant new industries and great cities, not model farms. By the turn of the century, Harris had become skeptical that any good could come from industrial progress—to him the phrase was merely a euphemism for materialism—and he escalated his attack on it. He believed that mass society, which followed in the wake of industrial progress, would rob the South collectively of its distinctiveness and Southerners singly of their individuality, a distinguishing trait of antebellum yeomen. Postwar Southerners, to their discredit, had become dedicated followers of fashion. For some of Harris's fictional characters "the old style [of living] did not fit the new times." They left their Middle Georgia farms and moved to Atlanta, deserting the old yeomanry for the new plutocracy.[36]

This desire to conform, to abandon regional distinctiveness, Harris perceived as the dominant force behind the New South's quest for industrial progress. As Uncle Remus says, "ev'ything is mo' samer now dan what it use ter be."[37] Harris treated the conformist impulse satirically in the animal tales. In one of them Brer Rabbit deludes Brer Wolf into thinking that an animal trap is a new kind of cradle that he must have for his children if he is to be considered stylish. Brer Wolf is then captured by Mr. Man, who had designed the contrivance to catch Brer Rabbit.[38]

Other of the creatures suffer even worse consequences. In "Brother Fox Follows the Fashion," Brer Rabbit, through the influence of Brer Fox's wife, persuades him that sleeping with one's head off is the fashion. Brer Fox's wife then chops off her husband's head, regretting only that there is no one to remove hers and make her fashionable. Even after she realizes what has happened she insists that her husband is better off dead than out of fashion.[39]

The heron's fate is similar to Brer Fox's. New to the swamp, he sees the other birds sleeping with their heads under their wings and thinks that they have removed them. Reluctant to be different, he summons Doctor Wolf, who obligingly snaps off his head. Uncle Remus, a product of the old times when fashion was regarded lightly, thinks this story a sad one and assumes the little boy will, too. But the child, Miss Sally's grandson, has been reared in postwar Atlanta where conformity is everything, and he fails to see the pathos in the tale. Harris agrees with Remus that some things should not be tried even once.[40]

Throughout the Remus tales, even those with the frame narrative laid in antebellum times, one finds comments critical of the postbellum ethos. Uncle Remus laments that, increasingly, values are based on money, that society cares little about how wealth is acquired, that the materialistic diminishes the mythic. He cuts through the pretensions of the boom-town Atlanta merely by the nonsense name he gives it, Lantamatantarum. He fears that Brer Rabbit, "a mighty man . . . when de creeturs wuz bossin' dey own jobs," would not "show up much in deze days."[41]

To Harris's dismay, the proponents of progress, despite their disclaimers, continued to praise the New Order and disparage the Old. In their view a community was nothing if not progressive.[42] Harris lashed out at this attitude. *Gabriel Tolliver* contains scattered authorial comments attacking the "restless but superficial minds, who mistake repose and serenity for stagnation." The quality of life in the village of Shady Dale, a place progress has passed over, is vastly superior to that in the growing cities where "the atmosphere of commercialism is unfavourable to the growth of sentiments of an ideal character."[43] Whatever the faults of the Old South, Harris maintained, fealty to "the Money Devil" had not been one of them.[44]

The New South has turned things over. As Uncle Remus tells the little boy, "ef de trufe wuz know'd we er stan'in' on our heads."[45] A sympathetically drawn character in *Gabriel Tolliver* observes that Southerners used to sneer at Yankees for their materialistic philosophy, but she believes that "it won't be very long before we'll beat them at their own game." More to blame than Radical Republicans for this change of Southern attitudes, Harris felt, were those native politicians who supervised the region's redemption from Reconstruction. Gabriel Tolliver perceives that "the champions of constitutional liberty . . . had their eyes on the fleshpots."[46]

In contrast to these real-life corrupters of the Southern tradition, there is the fictional character Billy Sanders, ideal yeoman and "garrulous half-brother" of his shy creator.[47] A prototype of the good old boy, Sanders is earthy and straightforward, discerning and wise. This level-headed countryman does not mind making a dollar, but he has only contempt for those men whose quest for money nullifies honor and principle. His comments on contemporary affairs deflate the pretensions of the South's new plutocracy. A favorite target for his thrusts is Colonel Augustus Tidwell, corporation lawyer, note shaver, and political chameleon, a man "who smacks his mouth ev'ry time he hears a nickel drap." Once a Greenbacker like Sanders and a Silver Democrat, Gus, alive to the changing currents of fashion, has enlisted in the forces of sound money and marches now under the gold standard. Principles blocking progress, he feels, should be cast aside.[48]

Colonel Tidwell is much admired by the local editor, for Gus is progressive, and to many of his fellow Southerners little else matters. Even the church realizes this. "Prosperity is one mighty good sign of Christ'anity," Billy has heard one preacher say. Though Sanders has never encountered that teaching in his Bible, he admits that the Scripture he reads comes from a sixty-year-old edition hopelessly archaic and unable to speak to currently perceived needs.[49]

However much Billy's progressive fellow Southerners distress him, he saves his most biting comments for the Boston capitalist visiting Harmony Grove to search for possible investments. The Bostonian is a bland and colorless fellow—not the stout, florid, side-whiskered worthy Harmony Grove expected—who mouths platitudes and has "apparently no views of his own."[50] The opinionated Sanders provides a refreshing contrast to the capitalist. This man, bent on exploitation, professes to have acquired a social conscience as, he says, have his fellow Northern businessmen who now believe that right and justice are more important than the expansion of trade and industry. Billy erupts: "You don't mean to say that after preachin' to we-all down here that trade and business an' money an' development an' commercialism is the mainstays of life, an' the hope of the nation—you don't mean to say that you're gwine to throw down your hand and drap out'n the game jest as we've begun to git a few chips on our side of the table!"[51] Billy dislikes the South's capitulation to Mammon, but he abhors the North's smug sense of superiority.

To Sanders, what others glibly style progress can be retrograde, yet he suspects that it is part of the natural order of things. If progress is inevitable, then sensitive men must chart its course, insuring that its result will improve the quality of life rather than foster a degenerate plutocracy. Harris's last novel, *The Bishop and the Boogerman*, makes clear his distinction between true and false progress. In that story, Billy Sanders supports the efforts of young John Somers to secure a right-of-way for a proposed railroad, feeling that this new means of transporting goods will benefit the farmers around Shady Dale. Somers faces resistance from Jonas Whipple, a miserly old reactionary whose reasons for opposing the railroad—among them, that the concussion created by passing trains will cause plant blossoms to drop to the ground—Harris treats as absurd. But if Whipple's position is unsatisfactory, so, too, is Somers's. Present-minded, practical, free of debilitating old prejudices, Somers is a decent enough fellow, yet he lacks the sensitivity of Sanders and of Adelaide Lumsden, the young lady he loves. His mind is so preoccupied with business matters that he feels no sentiment when he visits his mother's old home and sees the graves of his forebears. Modern life, moreover, has blunted his imagination. Only when his sensibility can transcend the commonplace, and when Cally Lou, Adelaide's imaginary childhood playmate and an old friend of Sanders, no longer feels uncomfortable in his presence, does Harris permit him to secure the right-of-way.

The world of business, Harris felt, seldom allowed its inhabitants to achieve this higher sensibility. Instead "the poison of money" had corrupted any noble sentiments they had ever had.[52] Wealthy businessmen, Harris wrote shortly before his death in 1908, "have closed their ears and their hearts to the appeals of justice, and fairness, and if [these men] have been singularly successful, they have lost some of the . . . finer feelings . . . that illuminated their youth."[53] These were the men who hailed progress, who spoke of the great advances of the age, but who, the author believed, were productive more of ill than of good.

In the last months of his life Harris made explicit his dissatisfaction with the results of the New South movement. An editorial in *Uncle Remus's Magazine* entitled "Progress—in the Best and Highest Sense" is laden with comments critical of what he believed to be the South's surrender to materialism. "We are in the midst of a sordid and material era," he wrote, in which "there is a great danger that many superficial minds will come to the conclusion that financial success is the main business of life."[54] The South made too much "unnecessary noise" over the "increase in the number of cotton spindles . . . which often represent the number of traps set to catch and smother . . . thousands of children, who are at least as important . . . as the amount of capital invested in the cotton mills."[55]

As an alternative to this South of misplaced values, Harris fashioned a myth of the yeoman South. This man who styled himself a "cornfield journalist" and "The Farmer" cultivated a fictional world significantly different from that described in the Plantation Tradition. The ideal society was the Putnam County of his youth, a middle-class arcadia of self-sufficient homesteads where men were judged on strength of character rather than on accumulation of goods, where even the bastard son of a servant woman and an itinerant laborer could profess to have suffered no ridicule. The yeoman South was the land of Billy Sanders, of men who felt themselves the equals of other men and to whom Harris could not condescend as Page did to Adam Rawson or Smith to Tom Yancey. Even the Negroes in this society possess a dignity and an individuality foreign to blacks portrayed by the plantation romancers; Uncle Remus and Aunt Minervy Ann are only distantly related to Page's Sam and Smith's Chad.

Moreover, unlike Page and Smith, who used the plantation myth to aid the cause of progress, Harris refused to press the yeoman myth into blind service of the New South crusade for industrialization and urbanization. Even though he spent all his life in the South, as Page and Smith did not, Harris more readily criticized things Southern, whether they were the region's chauvinistic literature or its unquestioning allegiance to the creed of progress. He could not, however, bring himself to disparage the yeomen, and ironically, it was middle-class Southerners—the people of Putnam and their kin—who were the heart of the New South movement. In many of them, there was little respect for the tradition that Harris cherished.

VII.

THE CRITICAL TEMPER:
MARK TWAIN AND THE
NEW SOUTH MOVEMENT

Because Samuel Clemens left Missouri as a young man and later, as Mark Twain, ridiculed the South's medieval romanticism, condemned its racial arrangement, and even satirized his own brief attempt to serve the Confederacy, he is sometimes not considered a Southern writer. But if Southern literature is defined so as to include only work lauding the region, it would be a poor and unrepresentative product indeed.

The ability trenchantly to criticize that resulted from the intellectual detachment enhanced by physical removal from the South— an ability the artistry of which exceeded that of Lanier, Harris, and all other postbellum writers—coupled with the pull of nostalgia, is precisely what makes Mark Twain the preeminent Southern author of the period. His relationship with the South, as Arlin Turner has pointed out, was "an affair of love and anger." If his denunciation of slavery in *Huckleberry Finn* and his unchivalric assault in *Life on the Mississippi* upon the Southern preoccupation with Sir Walter Scott stand out, conspicuous also is the extent to which his nostalgic recollection and imaginative amplification of his boyhood in the antebellum South drew from him his best work: *Tom Sawyer, Huckleberry Finn*, and "Old Times on the Mississippi." One part of him— Theodore Dreiser called him "Mark the Double Twain"—lamented what the New South of material progress was doing to his vision of the idyllic South. Consequently, as early as 1873, he attacked the inchoate New South movement in *The Gilded Age*. More so than Charles Dudley Warner, the Eastern editor who coauthored the novel, Mark Twain, backwoods humorist, supplied the social commentary of *The Gilded Age*, focusing on the "all-pervading speculativeness" and "shameful corruption" of postwar America, much of which was occurring in the South.[1]

Mark Twain's plot deals with Colonel Beriah Sellers, a likable ne'er-do-well whose ill-founded economic ventures always collapse, and with Sellers's friends, the Hawkins family. Silas Hawkins, native Kentuckian living on his 75,000 acres of supposedly rich but as yet unproductive land in the Knobs of East Tennessee, resolves to move to Missouri after hearing of the unparalleled opportunities there from Colonel Sellers, a dreamer who speculates in everything from railroads to sarsaparilla. Hawkins sets out with his wife, children, and slaves but before reaching Missouri adds two members to his household by taking in the orphans Clay and Laura.

Shortly after the Hawkinses arrive at their new home, Sellers persuades Silas to go into business with him. After a brief period of prosperity, during which Hawkins advances from his Tennessee title of "Squire" to that of "Judge," he falls upon hard times, suffering numerous bankruptcies. Judge Hawkins repeatedly considers selling the Tennessee land, but, believing it will eventually yield great wealth to his children, he refuses. When the judge dies, the obsession with the Tennessee land passes to his son Washington.

Meanwhile the Civil War has ended, a surveying party has entered the Missouri backwoods to lay out a railroad, and Colonel Sellers, his speculative enterprises interrupted by his service in the Southern cause, has resumed devising schemes to get rich and to develop the countryside. He interests the corrupt Senator Abner Dilworthy in the proposed railroad. Seeing possibilities for plunder in the project, Dilworthy agrees to help secure an appropriation from Congress. Before returning to Washington, the senator hires Washington Hawkins as his secretary and invites Laura Hawkins to the capital as his houseguest.

Still nursing the wounds of an unhappy love affair of the war years, Laura toys with her numerous suitors in Washington. She uses her beauty to full advantage as a lobbyist for Dilworthy, now interested in a project to establish on the Tennessee land an industrial college for freedmen. Colonel Sellers, whose railroad-construction and river-improvement plans have collapsed for want of funds, comes to the capital to assist Dilworthy and the Hawkinses in the fight to push the Knobs Industrial University bill through Congress. With success imminent, the bill is defeated when its sponsor Dilworthy is discredited for attempting to buy votes in his bid for reelection.

In writing his part of *The Gilded Age*, Mark Twain drew from familiar materials. The Missouri backwoods setting is a fictional rendering of the real Missouri of Sam Clemens's youth, and the Tennessee land also comes directly out of his experience, having belonged to his family for forty years. The characters, too, resemble people in Clemens's life. His father, John Marshall Clemens, provided the model for Silas Hawkins; Sam's brother, Orion, is Washington Hawkins. Abner Dilworthy is based on Samuel Clarke Pomeroy, senator from Kansas, whom Clemens had met in Washington in 1870. Colonel Sellers, entrepreneur manqué, is an adaptation of Clemens's cousin, James Lampton.[2]

Yet if Beriah Sellers was a reproduction of James Lampton, the colonel also bore strong resemblance to his creator Mark Twain, for whether he knew it or not, Mark Twain was as afflicted with the Sellers complex as any other man. In many ways a spiritual child of the Gilded Age, Mark Twain, like Sellers, delighted in the Great Barbecue "and wanted to carve great portions for himself."[3] As do most characters in *The Gilded Age*, he worshiped the golden calf. William Dean Howells recalled that whenever Mark Twain received a postcard telling of the proceeds from the latest performance of his play, *Colonel Sellers*, he would read the card aloud, brandish it in the air, and walk about the dining room exulting in his success.[4] Early in his career, he took to the grueling lecture circuit, motivated, at least in part, by a desire for material gain. To publish his own and other writers' books and to increase an already sizable income, he established the firm of Charles L. Webster and Company. Keeping step with the times, he looked to practical mechanics as a source of profit, experimenting with a perpetual calendar, with bed clamps to keep covers in place, and with fire extinguishers operated like hand grenades, and he invested heavily in James W. Paige's typesetting machine. How he made his fortune—whether through writing, lecturing, publishing, inventing, or investing—did not much matter. The main concern to Mark Twain, businessman, was to keep the coffers bulging.[5]

Like many of his fellows in the age of enterprise, however, Mark Twain did not know when to quit. The catalogue of Colonel Sellers's speculative misadventures anticipated Mark Twain's own financial reverses. Nothing came of the perpetual calendar, bed clamps, and fire extinguisher. After initial success, his publishing company began to suffer from too many titles and too little capital.

The Paige typesetter, though malfunctioning repeatedly, continued to obsess Mark Twain, and his investments in it became steadily greater. Stretching his resources to the breaking point, this writer who thought himself a capitalist, who was to associate with Andrew Carnegie and with Henry H. Rogers of Standard Oil, was forced ultimately to declare bankruptcy.[6]

Money fascinated Mark Twain as writer, too, though in a different way. As a man of letters he stressed the corrupting powers of the dollar. One part of him abhorred the postwar Trinity of "Gold, Greenbacks and Stock," "the true and only God," whose prophet was William Tweed. Reluctant to write about sex, Mark Twain in many works wrote instead what Justin Kaplan calls "a kind of pornography of the dollar."[7] His idea of money as the depriver of morality, evident as early as 1873, continued throughout his career, for it was money that poisoned Hadleyburg and Eseldorf. Mark Twain as writer, then, was outside postwar society, but as businessman he was in the thick of it. Consequently, when he satirized American speculativeness in *The Gilded Age*, he was also reading his own future and satirizing a part of himself.

The postwar South brought into sharp relief the all-pervading speculativeness and shameful corruption that Mark Twain and Warner chose as themes for their novel. Southern state governments, whether controlled by the Radical Republicans of Reconstruction or the Conservative Democrats who redeemed the region of Radical rule, provided ample illustration of corruption and speculativeness. The Radicals proved willing to fix elections, accept bribes, and use public funds for private purposes. The Conservatives, self-proclaimed models of probity, showed themselves rivals of the Radicals in many ways, even in tampering with state treasuries. As Mark Twain and Warner were writing *The Gilded Age*, the Conservative treasurer of Virginia was charged with embezzling state funds. Within a few years, other Southern states discovered their treasurers using public money for private speculation or simply disappearing with the revenue entrusted to their keeping. The speculative spirit in the postwar South found outlet in the extravagant railroad-construction and bond-issuing schemes of the Reconstruction governments. This spirit continued as Conservatives restored home rule, acquiring in the meantime the unwarranted optimism that was so much a part of the New South creed, and of the character of Colonel Sellers.[8]

Hawkeye, Missouri, the home of Colonel Sellers and the Hawkinses, was, like the Hannibal of Sam Clemens's youth, more a part of the South than it was of the West. In antebellum days, Hawkeye was slaveholding country, and during the war it supported the Confederacy. After the war, the people of Hawkeye in their pursuit of internal improvements behaved much as people farther south did. Mark Twain was on solid ground in portraying Hawkeye in this way. Postwar Missouri, in its attitude toward internal improvements, especially railroad construction, resembled the South more than the Midwest, where the Granger movement was heaping well-deserved abuse upon the railroads. During the 1870s, delegates from Missouri, promoting construction in the Southwest, flocked to railroad conventions throughout the South. When railroad builder Thomas A. Scott announced his intention to have an eastern terminus of the projected Texas and Pacific line at Saint Louis, Missourians applauded his decision, and later, when it appeared that this project might be abandoned, Missouri threatened to wreck Scott's entire plan by delivering its congressional votes to his opponents.[9]

Colonel Sellers is also unmistakably Southern. Having cast his lot with the secessionists, the colonel nevertheless wants to forget the war and forgive the Yankees, an attitude shared by many former Whig-Unionists who found a home in the New South movement. Moreover, the humor with which Mark Twain portrays Sellers does not conceal his resemblance in other ways to the deadly serious men of the New South persuasion. Like them, Sellers believes that economic regeneration in the form of internal improvements and industrialization is essential to Southern development, that the South must have Northern capital and federal assistance if it is to prosper, and that the exploitation of the South's abundant natural resources will of itself bring wealth to the region. Both Colonel Sellers and advocates of a New South actively engaged in trying to restore their region and themselves to prosperity and prominence.[10] C. Vann Woodward maintains that "it was more than a coincidence that Mark Twain selected the Southwest as the habitat of his Beriah Sellers. . . . Beriah Sellerses thrived there by the thousand in the seventies and their prayers ascended to Washington in the form of petitions, claims, and appropriation bills. Each of these bills and petitions embodied dreams of recouping lost fortunes, restoring the prestige of fallen family names, and sometimes the prosperity of whole states and regions."[11]

Colonel Sellers's dreams of getting rich and of developing backwoods Missouri materialize in a scheme to construct the Salt Lick Pacific Extension Railroad and to dredge Goose Run to make that stream navigable. Hoping to secure a congressional appropriation, the colonel presents a glowing description of the desolate region around Stone's Landing, a hamlet near Hawkeye. Goose Run, a mere trickle, becomes "the noblest stream that meanders over the thirsty earth." Slouchburg is the "noblest onion country that graces God's footstool." "There's dead loads of peat" under the swamps around Catfish and Babylon. The "sassparilla" in the area from Hail Columbia to Hark-from-the-Tomb is sufficient "to fat up all the consumptives . . . from Halifax to the Holy Land."[12]

Colonel Sellers's claims, though treated comically, exaggerate only slightly the celebration by New South promoters of their section's bountiful natural resources, healthful climate, and cheap labor. As early as 1869, a contributor to *De Bow's Review* wrote that the South's advantages would soon make "Nineveh, Babylon, [and] Rome, . . . with all their boasted wealth and dominion, sink into insignificance." Richard Edmonds called the land below the Potomac "Creation's Garden Spot," predicting it would be "the richest and greatest country upon which the sun ever shone." Henry Grady proclaimed that his region had God on its side, for "its prosperity has been established by divine law."[13]

An aura of speculation surrounds all of the colonel's enterprises, including his plan to develop the area around Stone's Landing. Sellers's project pales, however, when compared with schemes of nonfictional New South promoters. To place vast acres at the disposal of land speculators, New South enthusiasts in 1876 succeeded in persuading Congress to repeal the (Southern) Homestead Act of 1866. The economic development that advocates of repeal hoped would result never came, however; repeal succeeded only in reducing further the chances of freedmen and poorer whites to acquire land and in permitting outside interests to strip the Gulf states of their timber resources.[14]

Where railroad construction was concerned, dubious speculative enterprises often gave way to outright jobbery. For example, the Memphis, Pine Bluff, and Shreveport Railroad, "a replica of one of Beriah Sellers's pipe dreams," paralleled for 300 miles across Arkansas an existing line able to handle the traffic. Endeavors such as this indicated that what the New South wanted, in short, was plenty. It wanted the appropriations and subsidies with which Congress had surfeited the North and the West.[15]

Like the flesh-and-blood New South promoters, Colonel Sellers perceives that economic regeneration depends upon sectional reconciliation. Believing Appomattox irrevocable, the colonel is quoted as "heartily 'accepting the situation.'" He reflects the condition and the sentiments of many other Southerners when he says: "I'm whipped . . . the government was too many for me; I'm cleaned out, done for. . . . We played for a big thing, and lost it, and I don't whine." The colonel wants to forget the past, conciliate the South, and proceed with the business of making money. And so do the Yankees he meets in Washington, who look admiringly upon the Confederate brigadiers serving in Congress. Former enemies sometimes become comrades in speculation. Noting that the word "rebel" has passed out of use in the capital, a congressman's wife remarks: "My husband sometimes says that he doesn't see but Confederates are just as eager to get at the treasury as Unionists."[16] Old foes enjoy one another's company at the Great Barbecue.

Mark Twain fuses the themes of reconciliation and economic regeneration and brings them to bear upon the third basic idea of the New South creed—adjustment of the race question—in the passages dealing with the Knobs Industrial University bill. Though sponsored by Radical Senator Abner Dilworthy, the bill also reflects the bourgeois paternalism of many New South spokesmen toward the Negro. If he proved worthy, the black man, though by nature inferior to the Anglo-Saxon, should be given an industrial education that would enable him to survive in a competitive economy. Moreover, New South advocates reasoned, the labor reserve furnished by a Knobs University might be used in the industrial expansion that would surely come soon.[17]

The Knobs University bill falls victim to the same false optimism and blatant corruption that plagued Colonel Sellers's railroad and river project. To insure passage of the bill, its supporters resort to overblown language rivaling that later used by men such as Grady and Edmonds. According to one congressman, the college will be "a vast school of modern science and practice [combining] the advantages of Zurich, Freiburg, Creuzot, and the Sheffield Scientific." It will train the laborers needed to "develop [the South's] mines, build its roads, work . . . its fruitful land, establish manufactures." In no more than five years the prosperity brought to the South by the school will "pour untold wealth into the treasury." A New York newspaper predicts the "experimental institution" will "revolutionize the whole character of southern industry," doing for Tennessee "what the Industrial School at Zurich did for Switzerland."[18]

The hypocritical attitudes of whites toward the Negro repel Mark Twain even more than the exaggerations of the promoters. Colonel Sellers, though a racist, is at least straightforward in his opinion of the black man, preferring not to "disturb the niggro as he is." Smug Washington socialites, however, contemplate from afar the need to elevate "the downtrodden negro" and to turn his "erring feet into the way of light and righteousness." Among politicians this hypocrisy is particularly widespread. The corrupt Dilworthy's sanctimonious speeches on the white man's duty to help the Negro hide the senator's own selfish motives. Laura Hawkins observes that many congressmen say they support the Knobs University bill "simply out of love for the negro," but she knows that the prospects of plunder, of getting a share of federal subsidies, of placing friends and relatives in remunerative posts in the college provide the real motivation for congressmen supporting the measure. Fittingly, it is the exposure of Dilworthy's corrupt practices that kills the bill.[19]

Dilworthy, indeed, has no redeeming traits, and the flat portrayal of him is only one among many shortcomings of the novel. Almost every other character is either lifeless or stereotyped. Moreover, Mark Twain's central plot and Warner's secondary one are pieced together haphazardly, and Warner's contributions, especially, are rife with the bathos the authors criticized in other writers. But Colonel Sellers saves the novel from Mark Twain's inexperience and Warner's sentimentality. Of all the characters, only the colonel excites and holds the reader's interest. George W. Cable remembered James Lampton, the model for Sellers, as a man of effusive personality, good heart, and straitened circumstances, who claimed, in Sellers fashion, to have beer running from the faucets at his farm.[20] Samuel Clemens admired his extravagant yet unpretentious cousin—"a manly man, a straight and honorable man," he called him—and Mark Twain created in Colonel Sellers a memorable character of American fiction, a comic character, to be sure, but one surrounded by an air of pathos.[21]

Because of the author's artistic delineation of Sellers, the humor with which he is treated transforms *The Gilded Age* by a wonderful alchemy into a serious appraisal of postwar America. Although

Sellers is an elder kinsman of Smith's Colonel Carter, the relationship is distant. Both are treated with sympathetic satire, but it is significant that Carter succeeds in the postwar world while Sellers fails to improve his lot. To Smith there was no doubt that the New South was the good society, so he forces Carter to make a fortune in spite of himself. Mark Twain, however, had begun to suspect that the New Order fell short of his vision of the Old. It is as though Sellers fails because the postbellum world is not worth succeeding in.

And yet, until the end of the eighties, Mark Twain could profess to believe in progress. The course of human history, he felt, had been consistently upward toward the nineteenth century, the "worthiest of all the centuries the world has seen." In *Life on the Mississippi* he lamented the postwar South's affection for the "Walter Scott Middle-Age sham civilization, . . . the duel, the inflated speech, and the jejune romanticism of an absurd past."[22]

Mark Twain, the progressive, saw hope for the future, however. He detected in the Southern air "the wholesome . . . nineteenth century smell of cotton-factories and locomotives"; and even the old, supposedly indolent city of New Orleans he found "well outfitted with progressive men—thinking, sagacious, long-headed men." Nevertheless, he entered a demurrer. The New South also provided a congenial climate for men such as the drummers selling ersatz he saw near Natchez, "Brisk men, energetic of movement and speech; the dollar their god, how to get it their religion."[23]

Hank Morgan of *A Connecticut Yankee at King Arthur's Court* is such a man. By his own admission, he is "a Yankee of the Yankees," practical and unsentimental, bent on bringing progress to Arthurian Britain.[24] That Mark Twain makes Morgan a native of Connecticut transposed to sixth-century England does not conceal that at one level *A Connecticut Yankee* is a fable of the South.[25] Mark Twain makes explicit the parallels between Arthurian England and the Old South: slavery, an agricultural economy, and the code of chivalry.

Moreover, though Mark Twain may not consciously have intended it, England as transformed by the Yankee is an allegory of the New South of Grady and associates, who, like Morgan, try at once to be practical and theatrical. Whatever else New South spokesmen were, they were also showmen, impresarios staging the lavish productions in the form of the expositions of the eighties

and nineties. A major concern of Morgan, and of New South promoters, is the practical one of maximizing returns on investments;
yet at the same time they are all romantic idealists who believe
industrialization is the panacea for society's ills. As Hank Morgan
sets out to modernize medieval Britain, so New South spokesmen
worked to bring their land into the modern world. The prime symbol of the New Order both in Camelot and in Dixie is the factory.
Believing that technology will bring the nineteenth century to the
sixth, Hank Morgan builds man factories, teacher factories, and
even civilization factories. Like the Yankee, advocates of a New
South described the society they were trying to fashion as "less
splendid on the surface but stronger at the core" than its antebellum predecessor.[26]

But for all the unfavorable comparisons of medieval England
with Morgan's projected modern civilization, Mark Twain finds
admirable qualities in the Old Order. In some places, he attacks the
Arthurian aristocracy mercilessly, but certain knights of the Round
Table, though mindless by Morgan's standards, are nevertheless
noble. Significantly, their nobility diminishes when the Round Table becomes a stock exchange; then they behave much like Gilded
Age businessmen.

The ambivalence of the author toward the aristocracy is most
perceptible in Morgan's description of King Arthur, a depiction
drawing parallels, perhaps unconsciously, between the king and
the legendary Southern gentleman. Totally a creature of tempera-
ment and training rather than of intellect, the king cannot question
even the most brutal aspects of the social system over which he
reigns. But his training also instills in him his finest traits, noble
bearing and unwavering courage. When posing as a slave for a
tour of the country, Hank Morgan can take on the manner of a
menial, but Arthur, who disguises himself similarly, instinctively
remembers what he really is, and he cannot be changed by mere
outward appearance.[27]

The king, moreover, knows no fear. He possesses a special kind
of private courage, displayed in a smallpox-infested peasant hut,
that impresses the Yankee much more than his exploits in battle.
Whatever Arthur's faults, Morgan, echoing Mark Twain, comes to
believe that "there *is* something peculiarly grand about the gait
and bearing of a king, after all."[28]

In *A Connecticut Yankee* the cruelest feature of Arthurian England is the institution of slavery, presumably equated with the Old South in Mark Twain's mind. Yet when illustrator Dan Beard caricatured the slave driver of the novel he likened him to Jay Gould, not to a Southern planter, and that drawing earned Mark Twain's particular commendation.[29] Slavery, then, is seen as the oppression inflicted by industrial capitalism rather than by feudal agrarianism.

Mark Twain provides other evidence that his viewpoint is essentially one opposed to commercialism and chary of industrialization, a perspective deriving from his imagination's indebtedness to the envisioned Hannibal of his youth. In the first third of the novel, the author dissociates himself from the narrator. At this stage, the Yankee is merely a promoter, a showman, a self-server concerned only with how much something will pay. Mark Twain treats Hank's attempts to put Arthur's kingdom on a business basis with perceptible irony. Men, teachers, and civilizations cannot be produced in factories. But as the author fills out the character of Morgan into a crusader for social justice and political reform, he comes to identify with the Yankee. As Henry Nash Smith has written, "in proportion as the writer abandons his detachment and makes the Yankee into a mouthpiece for his own views, the protagonist ceases to be an entrepreneur in search of profit and becomes a humanitarian emancipator of the downtrodden peasants."[30]

All the action of *A Connecticut Yankee* looks forward to the day when Hank Morgan will have established his modern society and economy in Arthurian England. When that time comes, however, Mark Twain describes the New Order hardly at all, and, emblematically, this shows his disaffection with the New South. We do learn enough, though, to see the shortcomings of progress, for contrary to the Yankee's expectations, all is not well. The knights employed as railroad conductors appropriate the fares. Business duplicity occurs regularly at the Round Table, now a stock exchange chaired by Sir Launcelot. This former setting of chivalry has become a kind of Louisiana Lottery—an analogy Mark Twain consciously drew—that was promoted by two Southern knights, Confederate generals Jubal A. Early and P. G. T. Beauregard.[31]

The new industrial and financial order contains the seeds of its own destruction. Chicanery at the stock board is the catalyst for the Battle of the Sand Belt in which chivalry and modernity annihilate each other. Sir Launcelot turns the tables on Sir Mordred, Arthur's nephew, who has been trying to sell inflated stocks to Launcelot. Mordred then tells Arthur of Launcelot and Guenever's love affair. War results between the partisans of the king and those of the most respected knight. In the ensuing chaos the Church, Morgan's archenemy, gains control, places England under an interdict, and declares the Yankee an outlaw. Hank and his assistants take refuge in a cave surrounded by an electrified fence and defended with Gatling guns, benefices of the nineteenth century. Morgan's men kill 25,000 of England's knights but are themselves trapped by the corpses of their foes. Only Morgan, under a spell cast by the enchanter Merlin, escapes death to awaken thirteen centuries later.

Having destroyed knight-errantry and, allegorically, the Old South, the Yankee cannot create a suitable system to replace it. He therefore does not want to stay in the new age he earlier used as a model for transforming the old way. Mark Twain has prepared us well for Morgan's estrangement from modernity. Fairly early, he foreshadows the catastrophic conclusion by imaging progress as an inactive volcano, "standing innocent with its smokeless summit in the blue sky and giving no sign of the rising hell in its bowels."[32] As the story proceeds, moreover, "the contrast of civilizations drops from sight," the author instead directing his attack solely against the idea of progress.[33] At the end, Morgan feels "a stranger and forlorn" in the nineteenth century and longs to return to the lost land of his wife, child, friends, and "all that could make life worth the living!"[34] Unable to go back, he dies in despair.

A Connecticut Yankee marks a turning point in Mark Twain's development as a writer. Composing the novel intermittently over a period of five years, he did not systematically revise it, thereby enabling us to see his attitudes change.[35] The same writer who in *Life on the Mississippi* could express pleasure with what he called the wholesome smell of nineteenth-century progress could by 1889 detect the rotten stench of a decadent society. He turned his back on progress, lamenting an age not only gilded but hollow.

But there was always what Henry Nash Smith calls the "Matter of Hannibal": Cardiff Hill, the great river, Uncle John Quarles's farm, children like Tom Sawyer, Huck Finn, and Becky Thatcher.

"Mark Twain's genius," Dixon Wecter has written, "always swung like a compass toward his . . . childhood and adolescence in Hannibal."[36] To be sure, the town, as Mark Twain remembered it, was no place on earth; it was an ideal, a dream. But it was a Southern dream, an idyll innocent of cotton mills and blast furnaces.

VIII.

GEORGE W. CABLE AND
THE FICTION OF UPLIFT

In 1873, while Mark Twain was satirizing the nascent New South movement in *The Gilded Age, Scribner's Monthly* published a story, "'Sieur George," that many scholars maintain started the vogue of Southern local color in the national press. As Mark Twain became much more than a backwoods humorist, so George W. Cable, the author of "'Sieur George," moved far beyond the limits of local color to examine the shortcomings of the South's New Order.[1]

There was little in Cable's background to suggest that he would emerge as the most vigorous dissenter from the South's racial credo. Born in New Orleans in 1844 to a slave-owning family, he had served in the Confederate cavalry for two years, twice suffering wounds. But as he settled into work as a newspaper reporter and cotton clerk in New Orleans after the war, he read much, thought more, and, as he took up writing, began to deal with large social questions. Once convinced that the white South was treating black Southerners unjustly, he spoke out courageously in protest.[2]

Cable's earliest extended treatment of what was popularly known as the Negro Question or the Southern Problem came in his first novel, *The Grandissimes*, published in book form in 1880.[3] Set in Louisiana as French rule gives way to American control, the story contains obvious and, as Cable himself said, intended parallels to the post–Civil War South.[4] The Creoles who rage against the hated *Américains* may be seen as those unregenerate white Southerners who railed against the American government after 1865. These same Creoles' view of the Negro as an inferior being corresponds to the postbellum South's attitude toward the black man and receives the author's particular condemnation in the episode dealing with Bras Coupé, an African prince who prefers death to slavery. Cable contrasts the traditional Creoles unfavorably with another Creole, Honoré Grandissime, a progressive merchant willing to accept change, and with Joseph Frowenfeld, an American druggist who speaks for the author.

The contemporary relevance of *The Grandissimes*, however, was largely lost upon its readers.[5] To address the issue more directly, Cable later dealt with the Negro Question in essays and speeches, leaving no doubt as to where he stood. In an address delivered in 1881, he asked white Louisianans to be charitable toward the Negro.[6] Two years later, he showed that those people most often victimized by the convict lease system were black men.[7] Within nine months, speaking at the University of Alabama's commencement exercises, he criticized the white South for circumventing the rights guaranteed the Negro in the Fourteenth and Fifteenth Amendments.[8]

Subsequently revised and published as "The Freedman's Case in Equity," this address held that white men were legally and morally obligated to assure the Negro protection of his civil liberties in the voting booth, in public accommodations, and in courts of law. Cable refuted charges that he advocated the dread, undefined doctrine known to white Southerners as social equality. It was "a huge bugbear," he said, "a fool's dream."[9] Not he but proponents of racial segregation were promoting social equality, he maintained, for separation of the races tended to equalize all whites in one sphere and all blacks in another. Society's gradations were natural and acceptable to Cable, but they ought not to shut off the chance for advancement by the worthy or to follow the color line, which was arbitrary and unmindful of merit.[10]

Cable's tone was calm, but his creed was revolutionary, and it met with adverse reaction throughout the South. Probably no white Southern newspaper agreed with his stand. Robert L. Dabney claimed the Louisiana novelist and reformer had written "The Freedman's Case" for Northern money.[11] Paul Hayne, though he had read none of Cable's writings, called him a "renegade" and "a mongrel Cur."[12] The Creole historian Charles Gayarré, particularly angered by what he considered Cable's earlier affronts to the Creoles, vilified him as "a prodigious humbug, a phenomenal fraud, . . . a dollar scraper, . . . [an] insect."[13]

One of the few even-tempered replies to "The Freedman's Case" came from Henry Grady. Extolling white Southerners for their beneficent treatment of the black man, the Atlanta editor main-

tained that most Southerners, white and black, desired segregation because it enabled each race to follow its instinct to associate
socially with members of that race only. Grady, moreover, advised
the North not to be deceived by Cable's ideas. The number of
Southerners who agreed with Cable, wrote Grady, was minuscule.
The belief in white supremacy was an article of faith in Dixie; the
South was white man's country and would remain so. [14]

On that point, Grady was right. And Cable, though he clung
wistfully to his belief that there existed a "silent South" that felt as
he did, came to realize it. In 1885, partly because of the furor his
ideas fomented, he moved his family permanently to the North. [15]
By 1890, he perceived that the South did not intend to clean its
own house. Consequently, he advocated as a last resort federal
intervention to assure protection of the Negro's civil rights in the
South. [16]

Because the postwar South refused to guarantee the black man
his constitutional rights and was, in fact, devising duplicitous
ways to deprive him of them, Cable came to look uncharitably
upon the New South movement. For though tradition played a
part in shaping the white South's attitude, so, too, did the anes-
thesia of progress. He saw the New South creed's adjustment of
the race question for what it was: white supremacy and proscrip-
tion of the Negro. Though he could agree with Grady, Edmonds,
and others that Dixie's quest for wealth through industrialization
was a desirable goal, he believed the emphasis on economic progress was lulling the South into complacency toward social ills. Too
busy trying to get rich, the New South overlooked the injustice in
its midst. Humanity was being sacrificed for coke furnaces and
cotton spindles. [17] The difference in degree between Cable's attitudes and those of New South spokesmen was so great as to be a
difference in kind.

In *The Grandissimes*, a plea for social progress, Cable attacks the
business ethic. At one point, he observes that the businessman
never does anything gratis. Even his "pennyworths of thought" he
sees in terms of monetary value. [18] A passage in an earlier draft of the
novel, deleted because of wordiness, illustrates Cable's belief that
genuine progress and business values operate at cross-purposes.
Honoré Grandissime tells Frowenfeld that reform will not come to
Louisiana merely because of her entry into the American Union.
New Orleans will simply change from the military community of

the Creoles to a mercantile community, because businessmen will oppose progressive men on all fronts. Merchants and capitalists will stand firm against reform, for it is expensive and disruptive of the marketplace. All these men want, says Honoré, is "a steady *thrade wind* and they will sail for-h a centurhy over a stagnant sea and sweah, with the water-h in their mouths, that it is sweet and clear-h and good, all because they are-h afhraid [the progressive reformer] will rhaise the waves."[19] To Cable, Honoré's words were equally applicable to Louisiana and the rest of the South in 1880.

Dr. Sevier, another of Cable's novels with an antebellum setting, is also pertinent to the New South. The social import of the story is twofold: to counter the Cavalier myth made popular by the plantation romancers, old and new, and to intimate strongly that the New South has in some ways intensified the evils of the Old Order.

The setting is urban: New Orleans just before and during the Civil War. The characters are shopkeepers, a physician, a planter's disinherited son and his wife, some recently arrived European immigrants, and a few Creoles. The plot revolves around the efforts of the planter's son, John Richling, to find work, a task plagued by failure and frustration. There is nothing of the celebration of the old plantation and the Southern hotspur. The one briefly shown planter is portrayed unsympathetically as a stunted soul who disowns his son merely for marrying a Northern girl.

Richling's troubles result in part from an excess of pride that causes him to reject Dr. Sevier's attempts to help and from his inability to augment the plantation upbringing that failed to prepare him for life in an urban, materialistic world. But Richling is a good man, "amiable, quietly hearty, deferential, . . . [yet] self-respectful—and uncommercial."[20] He is more critical of himself than the author is, for Cable perceives that Richling's misfortune must be blamed largely upon the urban world he lives in. One suspects, moreover, that the society Cable has in mind is the New Orleans of the 1880s rather than the city of 1860.

The novel begins with a description of Carondelet Street, the city's business district, around 1880. The men who preside over affairs there seem to have sharper noses and keener eyes than anyone else. They are direct descendants of those merchants and capitalists who developed the district late in the fifties, "a sadly unchivalric grouping of men whose daily and yearly life was subordinated only and entirely to the getting of wealth, and whose every eager motion was a repetition of the sinister old maxim that 'Time is money.' "[21] John Richling is not such a man, and he suffers materially for it. Superior in every other way to the businessmen, he lacks the "knack," as his wife Mary puts it, for making money.[22]

After repeated failure, Richling eventually secures a situation as accountant for a baker. Significantly, his employer is not a Southerner but a German immigrant who puts little stock in appearances and is willing to give the impoverished Richling a chance. Grateful for this opportunity, Richling works hard. He plays by the rules, learns the way of the world, and in the process becomes a sadder man. He no longer cherishes old ambitions, for as he tells Dr. Sevier, "'my maxim a year ago . . . was to do what I liked. Now it's to like what I do.'"[23] His forced resignation to circumstance is even more pathetic than his former destitution.

Ironically, the job that enables Richling to earn a living is also indirectly the cause of his death. Eager to do well, he pushes himself past endurance and destroys his health. He is beaten down by the opposing ideals of the Old South and the New. On the one hand, the Plantation Tradition associated with the Old Order disdains work for gentlemen, and on the other, the commercial world of the city has little use for Richling's impractical learning and reserved manner. Caught in a cross fire, Richling has no refuge except in death. Cable's advice to the postbellum South is to keep a middle course, to honor the work ethic, but to resist the soul-numbing effects of materialism.

The commercial sensibility implicitly associated with the New South in *Dr. Sevier* wasted good men like John Richling by neglect. What was even worse, Cable believed, was that the New Order, in its single-minded quest for wealth, positively created some social abuses. The most conspicuous and brutal of these evils was the convict lease system. In the same year that *Dr. Sevier* was published, Cable delivered an address in Louisville condemning the inhumanity of this legalized torture. The raison d'être of convict leasing, he maintained, arose out of the South's desire to construct the artifacts of economic progress at minimal expense. But if the financial costs were low, the wages extracted in human suffering were exorbitant. The dividends of progress, no matter how substantial, failed to justify so great an investment.[24]

Yet, despite his exposure of the New South's blemishes, in retrospect Cable could write that as of 1885 he still held unconsciously to "the popular error that material gains . . . produce a general advance in civil and political thought."[25] The mideighties, however, were a watershed in his thinking. After the South's mean-tempered response to his proposed solution of the Negro Question, he came to feel that social reform does not of necessity follow economic progress. He believed that the development of the South's resources was desirable if that development served higher ends. It was clear to Cable that this was not the case in his native region.

The claim made by New South spokesmen that "material development . . . has . . . a political potentiality and can of itself solve . . . the Southern problem" Cable labeled absurd.[26] Echoing Honoré Grandissime, he wrote: "It is simply fantastical to expect a mere aggregation of private movements for the building of private fortunes to unravel the snarled thread of civil and political entanglements in a commonwealth."[27] Fortune builders, whether capitalistic colonizers from the North or native Southerners, were interested in making money, not in improving Southern society. The new plutocracy paralleled in some ways Cable's conception of the old plantation aristocracy. The old had long been decadent; the new was often corrupt. Both were socially irresponsible, elitist groups callous toward the lower orders.

Notwithstanding the bleakness of the Southern scene, Cable, long an optimist, cherished a slim hope that the picture would brighten. For there were always a few good men who did not judge others by race or family or wealth and who would try to show the South the wise course to an equitable policy. In time the South might heed their counsel.

John March is Cable's idea of such a man. He was not always so, however, and the story of his development from a headstrong, narrow, professional Southerner to a contemplative, broad, mature human being who lives in the South provides the nucleus of the plot for Cable's novel, *John March, Southerner*. Conceived in 1889 and published in 1895, this work prefigures William Faulkner's treatment of the South.[28] More than any other Southern writer before the great Mississippian, Cable, in *John March, Southerner*, attempted to portray the South's complexity, to show her strengths and her weaknesses. The material for the novel includes almost every aspect of the postwar South: attitudes toward public education, political and financial corruption whether occurring during Reconstruction or after Redemption, racial strife, individual violence, industrialization, railroad construction, colonization by European immigrants, and the boomer mentality of New South promoters.

To comment more directly upon the changes affecting the postbellum South, Cable used North Georgia as the basis of the setting for the story because the New South movement was much more evident in the Appalachian Piedmont than in the Louisiana Delta. Moreover, he had visited North Georgia early in 1890 and felt he could write of it with some authority.[29]

The story begins as the Civil War is ending and Confederate officers John Wesley Garnet and Jeff-Jack Ravenel are returning to Suez, the county seat of Clearwater in the state of Dixie. Major Garnet resumes his former occupation of minister and headmaster of Rosemont, a private academy and college for young men. Ravenel takes a position as editor of the local newspaper. John March becomes involved with these men when Ravenel learns of Judge Powhatan March's desire to send his son John to Rosemont. But the judge, like many nonfictional Southerners of the time, is land-poor. With few laborers to work his 100,000-acre Widewood estate, he struggles merely to pay the taxes on the place. Ravenel suggests that Judge March arrange for his son's education by using Widewood as security. John then attends Rosemont and is graduated, though his father's sudden death saddens the commencement ceremonies.

Upon leaving college, young March is a thoroughly orthodox Southerner. He views the Reconstruction government of Dixie as a refuge for scoundrels. Having suffered a brutal beating from a Negro as a boy, he dislikes and distrusts black people. His personality blends the conspicuously polite manner and quick temper commonly thought of as Southern traits. Priggish and self-righteous, March comes by his shortcomings honestly, for he has been too greatly influenced by his mother, a shallow, self-pitying poetaster, and by Major Garnet, who, we come to learn, is something other than the exemplary man of God he pretends to be.

Garnet is indeed a worldly cleric. Ostensibly to effect the economic revival of Suez but actually to enrich himself and a few associates, he devises involved and unethical promotional schemes. He is a boomer without equal, as extravagant as Colonels Carter and Sellers, but a cynic lacking their good intentions. Potential Northern investors who come to Clearwater County hear his perfervid descriptions of the area's inexhaustible natural resources. "There's enough mineral wealth alone," he tells the visiting capitalists, "to make Suez a Pittsburgh, and waterpower enough to make her a Minneapolis, and we're going to make her both."[30] As Cable observes, the "monologue became an avalanche of coal, red hematite, marble, mica, manganese, tar, timber, turpentine, lumber, lead, ochre, and barytes, with signs of silver, gold, and diamonds."[31] Garnet's grandiloquence is contagious, and soon nearly everyone in Suez is captivated by the illusory promise of instant and permanent wealth.

The Redemption of the state of Dixie from Radical rule and the completion of the Pulaski City, Suez, and Great South Railroad make the dream of riches seem ready for fulfillment. For Garnet's scheme to succeed, however, it must have the backing of John March because Widewood holds much of the area's considerable store of natural resources. Wishing to aid in the economic restoration of Suez and ignorant of Garnet's motives, March joins the Three Counties Land and Improvement Company, an organization formed by Garnet, Ravenel, and a few Northern businessmen. He travels to the North in search of capital to develop Widewood and to Europe for colonists to work in the prospective factories and to homestead on his great estate. While away from Suez, he becomes the victim of an intricate swindle perpetrated by Garnet and his unscrupulous Yankee associates whereby they secure possession of Widewood. March attempts to regain what was his, but Garnet's maneuver, it seems, has followed the letter of the law. Moreover, the people of Suez, "seduced in the purse," fear forfeiting prosperity too much to help March.[32] What they fail to appreciate is that the boom, based on Garnet's reckless enterprises, has already ended. For after Garnet and friends line their pockets sufficiently, they abandon development of the three-county area, leaving it a wasteland of unfinished projects, tied-up capital, and stranded labor.

Despite the misfortune that befalls March and Suez, the novel ends hopefully. By propitious circumstances, March secures proof of land fraud by Garnet, forces him to leave the state, and recovers much of Widewood. John spares Garnet criminal prosecution because he loves Garnet's daughter Barbara, whom he soon marries.

In time, March becomes the leading citizen of Suez, and as a result, the author predicts, the town will become a better place in which to live.

Notwithstanding the flaws of the New Order uncovered in *John March, Southerner*, the novel endorses the principle of material progress. But, as in his essays, Cable emphasizes again in this fictional work his belief that the South's economic advancement failed to move toward that higher ideal of an equitable social policy. Moreover, he doubts the substantiveness of the South's much-heralded economic regeneration. He refuses to accept uncritically the assertions of New South promoters, often viewing their claims as deliberate misrepresentations or as the products of wishful thinking.

In *John March, Southerner*, what the promoters contribute to the region are a groundless optimism, a disposition for pretentiousness, and a callous disregard for the South's most valuable resources—its land and its people. Although Major Garnet extols the white yeomanry of the three counties to Northern investors, this is merely a device to secure capital for industrial development. Cable contends instead that the South has virtually no middle class and that the yeomen Garnet celebrates are narrow, illiterate, and given to violence, the victims of a caste-bound social order.

If the promoters neglect the low whites, they act affirmatively to keep the black man in a subservient position. Garnet and associates think it high humor to have devised a scheme to siphon taxes marked for Negro schools into a fund to support the private institution of Rosemont. The blacks of Clearwater County have few friends among white Southerners but find a champion in the half-caste Cornelius Leggett.

It is through this mulatto that the author comments upon the Negro's place in the New South movement. Accused earlier of having idealized the Southern black man, Cable made sure no such charges could be lodged against this novel. A former slave of Major Garnet who rises to the state legislature during Reconstruction, Leggett lacks any semblance of morality in private life. He is a child beater, philanderer, and bribe taker. But even though he uses public office for private gain, as a legislator he zealously guards the interests of his black constituents. He agrees to support a proposed railroad only if the legislature will build a schoolhouse for every five miles of track laid and will construct a branch line to Leggettstown, a Negro settlement. Admitting that he is corrupt, he never-theless points to a major difference between himself and men like Garnet. "Niggers steals with they claws," he tells a political crony, "white men steals with they laws. The claws steals by the pound; the laws steals by the boatload!"[33]

In a conversation with John March, Leggett outlines his idea of what the New South should be. Comparing "New Dixie" to a chicken pie, the mulatto politician maintains that there "must be sufficiend plenty o' chicken-pie to go round." Blacks do not want all the pie, he says, but they do desire a fair share. To grant equality of opportunity to the Negro is, moreover, in the best interests of the white South, for "White man ain't eveh goin' to lif hissef up by holdin' niggeh down." Leggett's vision of the ideal South is not that of a white man's country or of a black man's country but of a poor man's country. He has a healthy class consciousness and, like some Southerners who supported the Populist party, hopes that through harmonious cooperation between the lower orders, black and white, a more suitable South will result.[34]

Even the so-called old-time Negroes in *John March, Southerner* know where their interests lie. After being freed, all of Garnet's erstwhile slaves leave Rosemont, notwithstanding his protests that he has always treated them well. They perceive rightly that the future holds more promise for them elsewhere. At another point Barbara Garnet's personal servant Johanna softly dissents as Major Garnet tells Northern capitalists that in Suez "Colored and white [are] treated precisely alike."[35] Later, when Leviticus and Virginia Wisdom, formerly slaves on Garnet's estate, are asked to serve at dinner, Uncle Leviticus, though as obsequious as always, makes certain they will be paid before he accepts the job. One cannot imagine Page's Sam or Smith's Chad leaving their old masters voluntarily, disagreeing with their social betters, or accepting wages for the privilege of waiting upon white men.

The difference is that Page and Smith were strengthening the stereotypes whereas Cable was attacking them with all the force he could muster. Cornelius Leggett is a character unique in nineteenth-century Southern literature.[36] Comical darky, "uppity nigger," and artful corruptionist though he be, he also fights in the cause of social justice. And Cable portrays him in the fullness of his hu-manity.

Only slightly less surprising than the picture of Leggett is the

portrayal of Major Garnet. Characters such as Gordon Keith and
Colonel Carter are exemplary men, as proper Southerners should
be. Contemporary readers did not expect prominent Southerners
to be presented as other than honorable. But Cable added a touch
of bitters to the saccharine brew of the literary Plantation Tradition.
If many Southerners found his mixture unpalatable, it nonetheless
contained more ingredients indigenous to the region.

Cable knew, of course, that most New South spokesmen were not
as coldly calculating as Garnet. There are characters in the novel
who object to his Machiavellian tactics. Even Jeff-Jack Ravenel, a
man who sits by silently as Garnet devises his scheme, objects to
the prospect of Northern capitalists controlling the development of
the three counties. He perceives that a colonial economy run by
Yankee financial buccaneers like Gamble and Bulger, Garnet's associates, will loot the South of its possessions. The mature John
March believes that economic progress should be a means to the
higher goal of an equitable society, not an end of itself. So, too,
does General Launcelot Halliday.

Halliday is a provocative character. Though many Southerners
of the time branded such a man a scalawag, Cable draws him
sympathetically and endorses his proposals for changing the South.
Of primary concern to Halliday is the deplorable neglect of the
land, the basis of the South's economy. To remedy this situation,
he hopes that bankrupt plantations can be reorganized as clusters
of small homesteads. He fears, though, that this will not occur
until the South abandons the crop-lien system, for this pernicious
arrangement discourages the immigration of industrious home-
steaders and stifles the ambition of native Southerners.

Though fellow townsmen admire Halliday's military record,
they reject his proposal for higher taxes to bolster Negro schools.
Speaking for Cable, Halliday expresses his conviction that the
prosperity of the South depends on elevating the black man. But
the old general doubts that reform can be effected as long as the
men who redeemed the South from Reconstruction are in power.

Halliday is a reformer who wishes to discard tradition. Cable
also wanted to reform and to nationalize the South, and yet he
loved deeply the land of his birth. In *The Grandissimes* Honoré
remarks that Frowenfeld finds "it easier to be in harmony with
Louisiana than with Louisianans."[37] So it was with Cable. In both
Dr. Sevier and *John March, Southerner*, he uses the phrase, "there is

no land like Dixie in all the wide world over."[38] He means this sincerely, though he recognizes that it is a sentiment too easily arrived at for many Southerners. The South is romantic, as John March says, but the romanticism, unlike the sentimentality of his mother's insipid poetry, Cable implies, is something spiritual, even mystical, an elusive feeling that only Southerners who love the South in spite of its blemishes can know.

Like Mark Twain's, Cable's relationship with the South was one of love and anger. What the region lacked, he felt, was the facility to criticize itself or to accept adverse criticism from others. When it acquired this ability, it might right the wrongs of its social system without forfeiting its distinctiveness. It might even show the nation how to fashion the good society. But as long as the South refused to examine itself critically, as long as it defiantly defended its social arrangement, as long as it lusted after the dollar without using it for higher ends, uplift would remain a fiction.

IX.

THE UNFULFILLED DREAM:
CHARLES W. CHESNUTT AND
THE NEW SOUTH MOVEMENT

Charles W. Chesnutt once inaccurately called himself "an Ohio novelist."[1] He was no more an Ohio novelist than George Cable was a Massachusetts novelist, or Mark Twain a Connecticut novelist, or Will Harben a New York novelist, or Sidney Lanier a Baltimore poet. To be sure, Chesnutt spent most of his life in Ohio, but he grew up in the South and the bulk of his fiction deals with that region.

Julian D. Mason, Jr., has written that Chesnutt was a Southern author "in the best sense of that term."[2] That is to say, he wrote *about* the South, not *for* the South. Unlike the plantation romancers, he declined to give Southerners the literary pabulum long served them. He refused to defend the region's shortcomings, hoping instead to excise them by facing them openly and presenting them realistically in his fiction. Like Cable, Mark Twain, Harris, and Lanier, Chesnutt at once loved and was angered by the South.

As the twentieth century opened, Lanier had long been dead, Harris's creativity was largely spent, personal misfortune turned Mark Twain's thoughts away from the South, and continued indifference to Cable's appeals led him to believe the battle for Southern uplift lost and to begin writing historical romances. Chesnutt, then, took up the task of critic of the New South movement, examining that movement from the perspective of the man most neglected by it, the Negro.

In 1866, Chesnutt's father, Andrew Jackson Chesnutt, was discharged from the Federal army at Fayetteville, North Carolina. Because his father lived nearby, Andrew decided to settle there and sent for his family in Ohio. Against his wife's wishes, they came.[3]

A boy of eight when he moved to Fayetteville, Charles Chesnutt lived in North Carolina until his twenty-fifth year. After studying at the Howard School, he became a teacher there at the age of fourteen. He amplified his formal schooling by reading avidly in the bookshop of a local white man and by listening to the stories told by patrons of his father's store. During the midseventies he taught in country schools in the Piedmont, returning to Fayetteville in 1877 to become assistant principal of the new State Colored Normal School. When the principal died three years later, Chesnutt took that position, having been recommended highly by the white leaders of Fayetteville.[4]

But the young educator, successful on his side of the color line, was dissatisfied. Though he could write in 1879 that the white people of Fayetteville were "very well disposed" toward the Negroes, he chafed under the distinctions arbitrarily imposed by racial segregation.[5] Of light skin, he had as an adolescent considered leaving Carolina and "passing" as a white man. In 1883, he did leave, but as a Negro, resolved, as he put it earlier, to help his race secure "recognition and equality."[6]

Authorship, Chesnutt believed, would provide a way to work for that goal. By writing fiction he hoped not only to fashion something aesthetically pleasing but also to serve a social purpose, to elevate white men by attacking "the unjust spirit of caste."[7] Within two years of his return to Cleveland in 1883, Chesnutt was publishing stories and sketches in the periodical press. Although these early pieces were often set in Northern cities, Carolina stayed on his mind. Consequently, as he continued to write he dealt more and more with that area of eastern North Carolina where he had grown to manhood.

The bulk of Chesnutt's fiction treats racial themes. His goals were primarily two: to shatter stereotypes of the Negro created by the plantation romancers and to present his readers with a new point of view—from the bottom of society.[8] He succeeds, largely through the character of Uncle Julius McAdoo, an old former slave who tells stories of life on antebellum plantations through a frame supplied by a Northern white narrator for whom Julius works in North Carolina. Like Harris's Atlanta Remus, Uncle Julius lives by his wits, telling stories not only because he enjoys doing so but also to secure material benefits. Through his tales he gains possession of an old building for fellow church members, gets choice victuals from his employer's wife, saves his nephew from being permanently fired, protects a chicken thief from prosecution, and shelters his own productive beehive.[9]

After being freed, Julius declines to leave the land where he grew up, but unlike the Negroes of plantation romance, he is no apologist for the old regime. As the white narrator says, Julius "never indulged in any regrets for the Arcadian joyousness and irresponsibility which was a somewhat popular conception of slavery."[10] On the contrary, even his fantastic stories of conjuration often attack directly the peculiar institution. The misfortunes that befall the characters in those stories and others occur because as slaves those characters have little control over their own lives. The author's point of view contrasts sharply with that of the plantation romancers whose Negro characters suffer only after they become free men.

In Chesnutt's stories, even the old-time darkies refuse to sentimentalize the Old Order. For example, Aunt Jemima Belfontaine, a white folks' Negro if ever there was one, states flatly that "Dem ole times wuzn't ev'ything dey wuz cracked up fer."[11] There is also the black vagrant whose preposterous tale of the glories of slavery fairly seeps with satire. This nameless old man recalls that as the manservant of Julius Caesar he had saved his master's life in battle. In gratitude Caesar gave him a quarter and promised to set him free at the age of one hundred. With a sigh the old man adds, "Ah, but dem wuz good ole times!"[12]

What were good old times to the plantation romancers were to Chesnutt "those horrid days before the war."[13] And, as he shows in his works dealing with the postbellum South, conditions had improved but little since the war. In one story, Uncle Peter, a freedman living in the Carolina Sandhills, resolves to build a place of his own. From the start his efforts are beset with misfortune. Having saved a little money, he buys fifteen acres of cut-over pineland from a Northern turpentine producer because no white Southerner will sell to him. Persuaded by another white man to buy a mule, Peter sharecrops with the man to pay for the animal. It is a costly year. A merchant overcharges him for supplies, rust gets in his cotton, and his mule dies. After paying off the twenty-dollar debt that the year's sharecropping brought him, Peter is forced to mortgage his land to meet legal fees for a son who has run afoul of the authorities. Still refusing to give up, the old Negro disposes of the mortgage and begins to build a house. Once he has erected the frame, a group of Ku Kluxers out for "a little fun" burn it, tying Peter to a nearby tree and making him watch. But the old man will not quit and resumes work on the house. The structure is almost complete when Peter, while working on the roof, falls to his death.[14] If the author stretches probability by the sheer number of Peter's reversals, each misfortune of itself is nevertheless credible.

Even more pathetic is the fate of Ben Davis. A hard-working, property-owning blacksmith in a small Carolina town, Ben is accused falsely of stealing by another Negro, Tom, who covets Davis's wife. After a halfhearted defense by his attorney, Ben is found guilty and jailed. Puzzled and dismayed, he attempts unsuccessfully to escape and is sent to the state penitentiary for five years. Upon release, he returns home, a broken man, to find himself forgotten, his wife living with Tom, his daughter drowned, and his son lynched. Shortly thereafter, he is killed by a white man who mistakenly thinks Ben is molesting his daughter.[15]

Although Tom is the catalyst of Ben's misery, the blame, Chesnutt implies, rests ultimately on a community too willing to forget Ben's accomplishments and believe the worst of him. Like Uncle Peter, Ben had tried to rise in the world, to do what friends of the black man said he must do to earn the respect of white men. But, according to Chesnutt, the one thing the postwar South despised more than a failed Negro was a successful one.

As portrayed in Chesnutt's fiction, the New South is a place opposed to the Negro's economic advancement. In the 1880s the white leaders of Patesville (Fayetteville) refuse to hire blacks to work in stores and factories. It is impossible for a Negro to become a doctor or a lawyer. The only way out of the fields is by preaching or teaching, professions that respect the color line and pay little in hard cash.[16]

If the Negro found it difficult to improve his condition in the postwar South, so, too, Chesnutt maintained, did the white man. Blaming the region's stagnation primarily upon attitude, upon the survival of the spirit of slavery, Chesnutt felt that the debasement of labor, the exclusion of Negroes from certain jobs, and the persistence of caste were hostile to progress for whites as well as for blacks.[17] Like Cable, he hoped that prosperity would serve the higher goal of an equitable society, would produce a "new order of things," in which men were judged upon character rather than upon color, family ties, or financial worth. [18]

Chesnutt envisions the ideal New Order in his last published novel, *The Colonel's Dream*. [19] Set in North Carolina in the 1890s, the story deals with the efforts of one man to bring prosperity, enlightenment, and human equality to his native region. A Confederate colonel at nineteen, Henry French moves to New York after the war and by middle age becomes the owner of a profitable burlap company. After his wife's death, French sells his business and returns to North Carolina, partly to restore his ailing young son Philip's health but also to see how his birthplace has changed. Clarendon of the nineties, he discovers, contrasts poorly with the town he knew as a boy. Trade languishes; the few industries exploit the people and the land; the very air reeks of decay.

Uncomfortable with his own success and the town's failure, Colonel French commits his fortune to improving Clarendon. He goes about building schools and libraries and renovating factories. These projects give work to the men of Clarendon, black and white. But in his attempts to make life better, the colonel collides with William Fetters, who, as his name suggests, binds others to his will. Of poor-white ancestry, Fetters is Chesnutt's idea of the new man of the New South. He is a prototypal Flem Snopes who exploits free white labor in his cotton mills, abuses black convict labor on his plantation, and intends to keep his grip on Clarendon at all costs. Fetters's henchmen work to inflame the local whites against French.

That task is made easier when the colonel violates the racial code. Though white men grudgingly work with Negroes on French's projects, they quit en masse when French replaces a defiant white foreman with a black man. From then on, the story of the colonel's plans is largely one of frustration and failure.

Along with reversals in the public realm, misfortune strikes French's private life when his son and his old black manservant Peter are killed in a train accident. Still, he strives to give substance to his vision until the white men of Clarendon exhume Uncle Peter's body from the French plot in the white cemetery. Angry and bitter, the colonel sees the futility of his mission and returns to New York.

The Colonel's Dream is Chesnutt's catalogue of the South's ills. As

Henry French fights convention in Clarendon, so his creator attacks the popular view of the New South movement and its leaders, singling out Henry Grady and denouncing him as a white supremacist.[20] He portrays the postwar South as a land sustaining and even honoring men like William Fetters while rejecting wise and farsighted leaders like Colonel French. Fetters is out to help himself; French, to help the South. The people they live among are too rooted in tradition to tell the difference.

The Southern traditions emphasized in Chesnutt's fiction were unrecognizable to readers of properly "Southern" writers—authors who did nothing but praise the region. To be sure, the postwar South, Chesnutt makes clear, received a legacy of graciousness, charm, and noblesse oblige. There are old aristocrats in his works who are admirable characters.[21] But Chesnutt's South is primarily a land of ignorance, indolence, and intolerance.

Despite the colonel's efforts to better Clarendon's schools and library, ignorance prevails. Even his offer to pay for improvements after his return to New York where he can no longer disrupt the town's social system avails nothing.

In part, Clarendon and Beaver County are backward because not only are the people ignorant but, unlike the white characters in Dixon's and Harben's works, they are lazy.[22] The men much prefer talk to work. Chesnutt's is not the leisurely South of the Plantation Tradition but a land made slothful, even shiftless, by the vestigial effects of slavery with its debasement of labor. The picture of Clarendon upon French's arrival reminds one of the squalid river towns in *Huckleberry Finn*. Cows graze on the main street; pigs wallow by the old market house; "lean and sallow pinelanders and listless negroes [doze] on the curbstone." Even the trees with "their rusty trunks and scant leafage [seem] to have shared in the general decay."[23]

And Clarendon is not alone. The town of Carthage forty miles away, though smaller, houses Excelsior Mills, Fetters's textile enterprise. Even so, Carthage wears "a neglected air." The men of the town spend much of their time at the depot watching the trains arrive. At the nearby mill village, while the women and children are inside the plant working amid lint and snuff drippings for as little as fifteen cents a day, the men sit languidly among dirty babies, swarming flies, and yellow dogs. But the South has a ready explanation for this condition. It lays the blame elsewhere—upon "the War, the carpetbaggers, the Fifteenth Amendment, the Negroes. . . . Effort was paralysed where failure was so easily explained."[24]

If the South is indolent, she is also, says Chesnutt, plutocratic.[25] Most residents of Clarendon admire and fear Bill Fetters. He is the poor boy who made good, having gained both wealth and the power that accompanies it. That he has done so by devastating the pine forests with turpentine stills and by degrading humanity in his mills and fields seems not to bother the people of North Carolina.[26]

According to Chesnutt's description of the advent of the poor whites, Fetters and his kind literally swarm out of the pine barrens, taking control of the state and implicitly of the whole South. As they come to power in the wake of war and Reconstruction, the South ossifies, subscribes to what W. J. Cash later called the "savage ideal," becomes intolerant of even the slightest deviation from convention.[27] A few of the old gentry fight a rearguard action but are hopelessly outmanned.

While the new men push the old master class into obscurity, they ruthlessly set about stripping the Negro of his humanity. On the weakest of charges, officials of Clarendon send black men to the tortures of Fetters's plantation as convict laborers. No breach of the racial arrangement will be tolerated, not even the burial of obsequious old Uncle Peter beside the white boy whose life he tried to save. For "such an example of social equality," says Clarendon's mayor, like Fetters a man of poor-white stock, might undermine "the purity and prestige of our race."[28] When Colonel French confronts such an attitude rapidly being institutionalized, he is bound to fail.

Despicable as the poor whites are, Chesnutt does not hold them personally accountable for their acts. As he has French say, "Environment controls the making of men."[29] The colonel is enlightened and progressive because he has seen the world, has lived in places other than Clarendon. By contrast, the poor whites know only Beaver County, a backwater of civilization. The Negroes, of course, receive not even the paltry benefits the benighted South has to offer.

There is one group of Southerners whom Chesnutt does hold accountable: the gentry. Though his novels contain some admirable aristocrats, his final judgment of the old master class is negative. Implicit in *The Colonel's Dream* is the author's belief that had the gentry deigned to associate with the lower whites, had they given them moral guidance, many wrongs of the postwar South—ignorance, prejudice, the worship of Mammon—might have been corrected. But the class schooled in leadership failed to lead. "The best people," Henry French says as he prepares to leave Clarendon, whenever "any deviltry is on foot . . . are never there to prevent it—they vanish into thin air at its approach. When it is done, they excuse it; and they make no effort to punish it. . . . [What] they permit they justify, and they cannot shirk the responsibility."[30]

Against the stone wall of society, the efforts of one man are for naught. The colonel's dream "of a regenerated South, filled with thriving industries, and thronged with a prosperous and happy people," will remain unfulfilled for many years to come.[31] In this novel Chesnutt offers no solution to the South's problems. Elsewhere he suggests that only sweeping reform under the aegis of federal authority will make the South a better place.[32] This, he admits, will not come soon.

But for all its faults—and Chesnutt spent most of his literary life writing of them—the South had a special hold on him. His fiction fondly describes the natural South: the majesty of the great pine forests, the loveliness of spring, the hauntingly beautiful sounds of night. Even Colonel French, an active, aggressive businessman, occasionally contrasts the bustle of New York with the leisurely pace of country life in the South where there is "no strident steam whistle from factory or train to assault the ear, no rumble of passing cabs or street cars."[33]

Like Cable and his character Frowenfeld, Chesnutt loved the Southern land. It was the South's people who enraged him. As the boomers raved of the region's inexhaustible resources, the New South's developers ravaged those resources, natural and human. Unlike Colonel French, whose farsighted plans would have developed the South without exhausting it, the common run of businessmen, devoid of social consciences, sought merely quick profits. Their abuse of nature diminished "their capacity for human emotion," a trait reserved largely for Chesnutt's Negro characters, who live on the land and respect it.[34]

To Chesnutt the capacity for human emotion, something the black man could contribute to the South, was just as important to the region as economic growth. What disturbed this fugitive Carolinian was that the white South, even the reputedly progressive New South, considered neither Negroes nor men like Henry French Southerners. Until the South developed enough to treat all its people honorably and fairly, the good society would remain a dream.

X.

OLD VIRGINIA AND THE
NEW SOUTH MOVEMENT:
THE VIEW FROM ONE WEST MAIN

The Colonel's Dream was the least popular of Chesnutt's works and had little influence in the South. Instead, some prominent writers early in the twentieth century voiced approval of the New South movement: Harben, Dixon, and Thomas Nelson Page, as we have seen. And there were others. Walter Hines Page, a native North Carolinian and a leading publisher in the North, set forth in fiction his belief that industrialization and education were curing all of the South's ills.[1] James Lane Allen leaned toward the view that moral advancement depended upon material progress. His fellow Kentuckian, John Fox, Jr., saw the pitfalls of progress, and yet Fox believed that Southerners somehow could get rich and "bring the old past back."[2] In a house at One West Main Street in Richmond, though, a young woman of good family and conventional upbringing was writing unconventional novels that treated the New Order with a skepticism lacking in much contemporary literature.

At the outset of her career, Ellen Glasgow appeared to have as her target "the inherent falseness in much Southern tradition," engendered by what she called "the philosophy of evasive idealism." Resulting from what she felt was the shallowness of the antebellum South's culture and the region's enslavement to the Lost Cause, evasive idealism fostered an unwillingness to face the harsh realities of the postbellum era. Mired in sentimentality, Southern writers, she believed, were failing to struggle against this suffocating attitude. As for herself, she vowed to treat "those ugly aspects of life the sentimentalists passed over."[3]

And she did. In the six novels set in postbellum Virginia written before 1914, one finds instances of infidelity, fornication, bastardy, miscegenation, murder, drunkenness, embezzlement, and attempted lynchings.[4] Although she failed to deal with such matters as explicitly as did later Southern novelists, what is striking is that they appear at all. No doubt many other people could agree with her older kinsman who averred that proper Southern girls should not even know what bastardy was and certainly should not be writing about it.[5]

Surely little in Ellen Glasgow's familial surroundings nurtured her early revolt against convention. Her boorishly practical father Francis Thomas Glasgow, the manager of Richmond's Tredegar Iron Works, viewed with misgivings her interest in the life of the mind. Her mother, Anne Jane Gholson, of Tidewater gentry connections, was sickly, sad, and self-absorbed. Like other proper young ladies, Ellen attended dances at nearby colleges and "came out" in Richmond society.[6]

But unlike most other debutantes, Ellen Glasgow read, and she read more than sentimental romances. She studied Darwin, the German philosophers, the great English novelists from Fielding to Hardy, and the French realists. What reading and reflection gave her were an appreciation of life as process, as change, and a reluctance to embrace the facile optimism of the age.[7]

Her reading helped direct her writing, and she was, as she herself said, a born novelist. In 1880, during her seventh year, she wrote her first sketch, and before reaching eighteen she had completed 400 pages of a novel she subsequently destroyed. By 1913, at age forty, she had published ten novels and a book of poems.[8]

Because her native state was what she knew best, most of these novels are set in Virginia. Their tone is almost uniformly somber because of her intellectual grounding, personal misfortune, and belief that little in Virginia warranted optimism.[9] The central characters, even when they can act, usually face life resigned to the worst—and often get it. Nicholas Burr in *The Voice of the People* is killed trying to stop a lynching, Christopher Blake in *The Deliverance* and Daniel Ordway in *The Ancient Law* spend time in prison, Ben Starr in *The Romance of a Plain Man* is nearly overwhelmed by his quest for money and power, and Virginia Treadwell in *Virginia* is deserted by her husband. In the end these characters seldom prevail over circumstances; more often, they merely endure them. And they endure despite their surroundings and because of some inner fortitude.

Much of what Ellen Glasgow found wrong with postbellum Virginia, as expressed in her letters and essays, she traced to the "tyranny of tradition." Fashioned out of sentimentality, the legend of the Lost Cause, she wrote in the 1930s, had a "stranglehold on the intellect." The Old South's legacy of "imperishable charm" failed to suffice for the new age. The inability to adjust to a changing world made the aristocratic tradition, quite simply, irrelevant.[10]

In the earlier novels, though, the decline of the Old Order serves less as a theme in its own right than as a counterpoint to the rise of the yeomen, or, as Glasgow called them, the plain people. She considered their advance the most significant development of the postbellum years.[11] Seldom, however, does she depict this development against the backdrop of industrialization. By and large, novels dealing specifically with the rise of the middle class, such as *The Voice of the People*, *The Deliverance*, and *The Miller of Old Church*, have rural settings. *The Ancient Law*, though set partly in a mill town, is more a psychological novel than a social one, describing the new industrial order but infrequently and vaguely. Only in *The Romance of a Plain Man* and in the first part of *Virginia* does the New South movement receive direct and sustained treatment.

"The significant drama," Ellen Glasgow wrote of *The Romance of a Plain Man*, "is the drama of external occurrences."[12] More so than for any of her previous Virginia novels, this assessment holds true. Although, as a novelist writing social history, she usually gave milieu great importance, setting is crucial to *The Romance of a Plain Man*, for were it different the novel could not have been the same kind of story. That is to say, setting serves to shape the action more in this novel than in those laid in rural surroundings. Appropriately for a story treating the changes wrought by the New South, the scene is Richmond from the 1870s to the first decade of the twentieth century.

Although Richmond's age and sense of propriety saved it from some of the excesses of boomerism, it nevertheless participated fully in the industrial activity of the time. With plants that had produced matériel for the Confederacy converted to peacetime operation, Richmond was one of the few Southern cities where factories were more important than marketplaces and where "the industrial ethic of the New South first took hold." Tobacco processing, metals manufacturing, and commerce dominated its economy. It was home for some 800 salesmen pushing their products throughout the Southeast. Between 1889 and 1891, promoters spent $12 million in real estate development. In fine New South fashion, the city sponsored an industrial and agricultural exposition in 1888 that drew as many as 30,000 people a day. It boasted of operating "the first practical electric street cars in the world."[13]

Into such an environment enters Ben Starr, the protagonist of *The Romance of a Plain Man*. The son of a stonecutter living in Church Hill, a run-down section of Richmond, Ben leaves home as a boy when his father, a widower, remarries. Finding work as delivery boy for a vegetable vendor, by chance Ben meets General George Bolingbroke, industrialist, banker, and president of the Great South Midland and Atlantic Railroad, who, to silence the boy's entreaties, gives him a job running errands in his tobacco factory. Hard work and an evident attempt at self-improvement gain Ben the general's favor, and as a young man he becomes assistant to Bolingbroke. Ben learns the ways of business quickly. Shrewd speculating earns him a fortune of $50,000 well before he reaches thirty.

Financially secure, Ben seeks and wins the hand of Sally Mickleborough, an aristocratic young lady of character whose ancestors include the families of Bland and Fairfax. Despite the opposition of Sally's maiden aunts who, as her guardians, believe the match beneath her and despite Ben's compulsion to work that keeps him too much away from home, their love endures. Security, however, is transitory, for Ben loses his money during a panic when the bank of which he has become president suffers a run. Broken in spirit and health, he is taken ill and is bedridden for a time. Because her husband is with her more, Sally enjoys their reduced circumstances, even though, to earn money, she is forced to launder and bake for others.

Upon recovery, Ben once again neglects his wife for his work. While he is busily recouping his fortune through railroad ventures, Sally, after the death of their small son, seeks diversion in the company of young George Bolingbroke, the general's nephew. Ill at ease in upper-class society and obsessed with business, Ben declines their invitations to join them for entertainment.

Just as Ben, upon the general's retirement, is offered the presidency of the Great South Midland and Atlantic, his lifelong ambition, Sally is stricken with a malady that requires constant care and residence in an appropriate climate. Perceiving love and duty as more important than wealth and power, Ben, as the story ends, declines the presidency of the railroad and prepares to take Sally to southern California.

Glasgow scholars have noted her painstaking attention to verisimilitude in *The Romance of a Plain Man*, and much of the novel is good history indeed.[14] Because the postbellum South was a fluid society, new men like Ben Starr could make their way up, though often the task was a difficult one. When they reached the top, they sometimes found men like General Bolingbroke already there: antebellum aristocrats and Confederate leaders who adapted quickly to the new dispensation. Linking the fortunes of Ben and the general with the railroad is also appropriate, for this was a time of feverish expansion in that industry.

Ben Starr finds much to admire in the New Order. For him it is a time of vitality and promise, with democratic ideals displacing the Old World tradition of antebellum days. It is a time that allows him to take part in "the joy of the struggle" to achieve. It is a time when "the claims of tradition . . . yield . . . to the possession of power."[15]

But Ben, though the narrator of the story, is not Ellen Glasgow. If she, as he did, favored the loosening of restraints that for too long had kept down able men of the lower classes, she found repugnant the motivating force in Ben's life—his belief that the mettle of a man is the achievement of material success. Even so, considering the nature of the times, Glasgow asks implicitly, how else can Ben be expected to feel? Did not the New South value success above all else? If a man were smart, was he not also rich?

There are irony and pathos in Ben's plight. He resents the snobbery of aristocratic relics like Sally's aunt, Miss Mitty Bland, and yet, the purpose of all his striving is not so much to make money for the sake of being wealthy as to use the power that accompanies wealth to secure acceptance by the very gentry among whom he feels so uncomfortable. Still, however much he excels, Miss Mitty and her kind will merely tolerate him; they will never accept him.

For all his success, Ben cannot master the art of living. Unlike the truly civilized characters of other early Glasgow novels—such as Tucker Corbin, the reduced aristocrat in *The Deliverance*, and Reuben Merryweather, a plain man in *The Miller of Old Church*—who live on the land and esteem nature more than social conventions, Ben fails to find satisfaction. Only when he can properly order his values and perceive that his goal is unworthy of the striving and that life is a great deal more than work does he have the prospect of contentment.

Paradoxically, the new man Ben is bound slightly less securely to the materialist ethic than is General Bolingbroke. Though at one point Ben thinks his own triumph would signal the overthrow of the general's values, he and Bolingbroke want the same things: money and power. A steadfast apostle of the gospel of work, the general believes that sweat and "hard pushing" are the means to success and thinks there is "more lasting honour in building a country's trade than in winning a battle." He admires Ben's rise, scorning the closed society that would prevent it.[16]

Proud of his success in rejuvenating the Great South Midland and Atlantic after the war, the general, relishing the power of his position, uses it willingly to make the road even larger. The Great South Midland and Atlantic survives the panic that breaks Ben and forces some of the general's competitors to the wall, causing Bolingbroke to exult that his line is the most "solid road in the country" and that "it's growing—swallowing up everything that comes in its way, like a regular boa constrictor."[17] Later, when Ben is trying to make a second fortune by carrying coal from West Virginia mines, he asks the general to lend him some cars. The general provides them but shows that he sees the possibilities of the situation when he tells the younger man: "If you weren't a friend, this would be a mighty good chance to squeeze you; . . . we could keep your cars back until we'd clean squelched your traffic, and then buy the little road up for a song."[18] Although the general acknowledges that such an act is unfair, the implication is that any carrier not fortunate enough to be his friend should beware.

The general has convinced himself and others that his motive has been primarily to help the South, not to enrich himself. To be sure, there is an element of altruism in his makeup, for he desires to be remembered simply as one who "brought help to the sick land."[19] Fundamentally, though, he immerses himself in business because that is all he can do. Even Ben can see this when he reflects: "The romance of . . . [the general's] life . . . was not a woman, but a railroad, and his happiest memory was . . . the day when the stock of the Great South Midland and Atlantic had sold at 180 in the open market."[20] Though adventurous, the general's life has been largely loveless. Ben finally rejects the materialist ethic for love; the general does not.

Bolingbroke had loved once in his youth, but the object of that love, Miss Matoaca Bland, Sally's feminist aunt, had too independent a mind to suit him, and the relationship deteriorated. Much as he might scoff at the "nonsense" of the Mitty Blands, he recognizes his kinship with that breed and can say to Ben that "something considerably worse" than useless tradition is independent thinking.[21]

If the general considers much of the gentle tradition ridiculous, there is one aspect of it that he admires. People like the Blands have a certain style wanting in others. "What they're proud of," the general tells Ben, "is that they can do without . . . [material] things; they've got something else—whatever it is—that they consider a long sight better."[22]

That "something else" is personified in Sally. Disdaining snobbery, she uses her mastery of the social graces to put others at ease in what could be embarrassing situations. Throughout their relationship Ben remains amazed at her charm and graciousness. She has, besides, a more important quality alien to him: the ability to laugh at adversity. When Ben's financial ruin forces them to adjust their way of living, Sally responds not bitterly but cheerfully. As Ben agonizes over her washing and cooking for others, she delights in the opportunity to be useful, to be something other than a mere social ornament. Even though Ben himself lacks Sally's fortitude, he recognizes it in her: "This humour, this lightness, and above all this gallantry, which was so much a part of the older civilisation to which . . . [Sally] belonged, wrought upon my disordered nerves. . . . Here, at last, I had run against that 'something else' of the Blands', apart from wealth, apart from position, apart even from blood."[23] Significantly, when Ben begins amassing his second fortune, Sally feels diminished. It is as though the ambience of the New Order stifles admirable people such as she.

Ellen Glasgow's picture of how the postbellum ethos affects her characters is sharp and clear. The main flaw in the novel results from her use of the first-person narrator. She worked best when the focus of narration was that of the omniscient author. Moreover, her choice of Ben Starr as narrator compounds the error, for she was hardly equipped to speak through a tycoon. Consequently, Ben's language sometimes rings false, and the novel lacks the realistic detail of, say, Dreiser's Cowperwood trilogy.[24] What is pertinent here, though, is not so much expertise of execution but intent. Far from lacking the "skepticism . . . broad enough to include the Brave New South" attributed to some of her early work, *The Romance of a Plain Man* demonstrates her conviction that the materialist ethic was hardly a suitable alternative even to a heritage of intellectual ossification.[25]

One can find a stronger indictment of the industrial ethic in the first book of the three that comprise the novel *Virginia*. The central theme of this story, unlike that of *The Romance of a Plain Man*, is the inadequacy of romantic love to sustain a relationship. After the first section, this topic absorbs Glasgow's attention, and the action increasingly becomes domestic, tracing the lives of Oliver Treadwell, an aspiring playwright, and Virginia Pendleton, a sweet, old-fashioned Southern girl, from courtship through twenty years of marriage to separation when Oliver leaves Virginia for another woman. For the first 200 pages, though, Glasgow is concerned with depicting milieu.

As with *The Romance of a Plain Man* her choice of scene is fitting. A small city of some 20,000 people in the mideighties, Dinwiddie, Virginia, is a fictional rendering of Petersburg. Like nearby Richmond, Petersburg felt the effects of the New South movement, having a real estate boom of its own marked by "unreasonable land speculation."[26] The city was home for such people as the gentleman of old family who advised his fellow townsmen to "be a part of the New South . . . which is even now [in 1887] rousing itself like a young lion from past listlessness."[27]

The man responsible for awakening the sleepy city of Dinwiddie is Oliver's uncle, Cyrus Treadwell, tobacco manufacturer, railroad builder, and complete materialist. Everything Cyrus does is designed to turn a profit. He is at once a less sympathetic and a better drawn character than Ben Starr, possessing an "intransigent reality . . . lacking in Ben."[28] The author describes Cyrus variously as a man "of small parts and of sterile imagination," "soulless as a steam engine," "a defeating force." He bullies his wife, refuses to send his daughter to college, lies with a Negro laundress, and derides his nephew's desire to write plays. If Oliver must write, Cyrus suggests he do an inoffensive history of Virginia that would be used in the schools, thereby making money for its author.[29]

Many other Dinwiddians agree with Cyrus that making money is far more important than anything else, for Cyrus is greatly praised. One of his staunchest admirers is Miss Priscilla Batte, headmistress of Dinwiddie's Academy for Young Ladies, whose sole qualification to teach is that her father, a Confederate general, fell heroically at Gettysburg. Though Miss Priscilla might fail to excite the intellectual curiosity of her students, she assiduously trains them in proper conduct, weeding out eccentricity. Like Cyrus, she believes that if Oliver must write he should write history, "a good history of the war—one that doesn't deal so much with the North." Unable to conceive an idea, Miss Priscilla clings "passionately to the habits of her ancestors under the impression that she [is] clinging to their ideals."[30] Like many other Dinwiddians, Miss Priscilla is a provincial chauvinist, so whatever brings renown to the town receives her warmest praise. As a result, she can proclaim Cyrus a great man because she perceives but dimly that such as he are the agents of change, "for so obscure was her mental connection between the construction of the future and the destruction of the past, that she could honestly admire Cyrus . . . for possessing the qualities her soul abhorred."[31]

But the change wrought by New South industrialists, Ellen Glasgow suggests repeatedly, might be only superficial. For Old South, as seen in Miss Priscilla, and New, as depicted in Cyrus, have much in common: both suspect learning, disdain art, ignore such problems as race, and worship "the illusion of Success."[32]

Priscilla Batte typifies one angle of Ellen Glasgow's vision of the aristocratic tradition. Her assessment of that tradition is modified when personified by the Pendletons: Virginia, her mother, and her father Gabriel, Confederate hero and Episcopal rector. Not their intellects, which unhappily are stunted, but their feelings, the product of tradition, govern their actions. And their feelings are good ones, for the Pendletons have the capacity to love. They are selfless people; they give, whereas Cyrus takes.

In the characterizations of Gabriel and Cyrus, Glasgow forcefully contrasts Old and New. Gabriel's most serious flaw is his lack of intellectual toughness; he wants the critical vision.[33] Even so, he knows in his heart that Cyrus's way is wrong, that the leech of commercialism has sucked him dry. For his part Cyrus is contemptuous of Gabriel's softness, but it is that very quality that makes the rector an admirable man. Compassion leads him to devote his life to serving others, even to death, for he is killed preventing a lynching.

Although Virginia herself, as Marion K. Richards has shown, was ironically conceived, as the story unfolds she increasingly becomes a sympathetic character. She is good, perhaps too good for an imperfect world, but, as the author intimates, that is society's failing, not Virginia's. By the end of the novel, as Louis D. Rubin, Jr., has written, "one has the conviction that . . . it is not Virginia's old-fashioned values that are at fault, but those of the crass new times."[34]

The treatment of the New South in *Virginia* foretold Ellen Glasgow's growing disillusionment with the New Order. If there were aspects of the Old Order that deserved discarding, "a mushroom plutocracy" scaling "the national Babel" was hardly a suitable replacement. As her friend Stark Young wrote in 1930, "To mix her up with the industrialization of the South . . . is a mistake."[35] And to associate her with the New South movement in the heady atmosphere of the turn of the century unjustifiably diminishes her acumen as social critic. Much was wrong with the New South, and Ellen Glasgow told about it.

EPILOGUE:
THE ROAD TO THE RENASCENCE

Anyone reading Page, Smith, Dixon, or Harben early in the twentieth century could not have discerned that the New South movement was hardly the success its spokesmen claimed. Caught up in
the euphoria of progress, these writers, even as some of them
nurtured the legend of the plantation South, endorsed the new
ideology, exaggerating its accomplishments. To these literary supporters of the New South movement, it signaled a victorious
South, respected by the nation, recapturing the eminent position
in national affairs it had once enjoyed, and all the while sustaining
the myth of the aristocratic Old South. The South must be the
best—judged by the standards of others. What they envisioned
was the South Triumphant, even though, were their vision to come
true, the South might not still be the South. Virtually without
qualification, they sanctioned the new ideology, which proclaimed
that the South could excel under the new ethos and still retain its
distinctiveness. They would at once build factories and restore
mansions peopled by the old gentry or by the new bourgeoisie to
whom they imparted aristocratic qualities, who would get rich by
sharp business and at day's end trace their illustrious genealogy.

But certain other Southern writers, though they might feel at
times that they should endorse the New Order, could not finally
do so. It went too much against the grain of Southern myth and
experience, against the image of the South as arcadian alternative
and pastoral rebuke that was their intellectual inheritance. If the
literary detractors differed on precisely what constituted the good
society—some found it in the aristocratic myth, others in the yeoman myth, still others in the hope of a racially egalitarian South—
they all agreed on what the good society was not. It was not a
society formed around the industrial impulse, an impulse that de-
humanized the individual and atomized the community. They
cherished what David M. Potter has called the folk culture with its
personalism in human relations lacking in industrial society, a culture in which one's life had a "relatedness and meaning" absent

from mass culture.[1] The New South movement, these writers feared, would destroy the Southern gemeinschaft, which could exist only in a rural or village environment. Harmony Grove would become Commerce, with all the pernicious ramifications that the name change of that Georgia town signified.[2]

The opponents of the new industrial ideology sustained the pastoral tradition in Southern letters and bequeathed it to the more talented writers of the Southern Literary Renascence beginning in the 1920s. The writers of the 1880s and those of the 1920s—Faulkner, Wolfe, the Agrarians—were working in quite similar social milieus. If the New South fever induced delirium in the eighties only to abate somewhat amid the agrarian unrest of the nineties, it never really subsided, and after the First World War it reached temperatures even higher than those that followed Reconstruction.[3] Fittingly, Henry Grady's old hometown was the chief locus and prime symbol of the enthusiasm, second phase. As George B. Tindall has observed, the "Atlanta spirit reigned supreme in the Babbitt warrens of the New South." If there was more substance to the industrial-urban growth of the twenties than to that of the eighties, there was also even more ballyhoo. Boosterism was rampant from Florida's Gold Coast to Asheville's Land of the Sky.[4]

At least one Asheville native did not like it. By the midtwenties Thomas Wolfe's birthplace was, in his opinion, "Boom Town, where everyone is full of Progress and Prosperity and Enterprise, and 100,000 by 1930, and Bigger and Greater Asheville." What the promoters meant by progress, said Wolfe, was "more Ford automobiles [and] more Rotary clubs," the glory of it all trumpeted by "cheap Board of Trade boosters, and blatant pamphleteers."[5] He was "keenly aware that industrial progress and the things associated with it could have damaging effects on . . . southern culture."[6]

Throughout *Look Homeward, Angel* Wolfe deflates the booster mystique. In scene after scene he derides the materialist ethic: Luke Gant, hawking home lots, ranting of Altamont's mineral resources—"gold, silver, copper, iron, bituminous coal and oil, will be found in large quantities below the roots of all the trees"; Hugh Barton, businessman, "selling" himself by getting "the other fellow's psychology"; Eliza Gant, waxing wealthy from real estate deals, yet too stingy even to eat right.[7]

The revolt-from-the-village motif pervades the novel because to Wolfe Altamont is a gesellschaft in microcosm. Society is fragmented, mechanistic. Everyone is split off. All life is subsumed to the passion of getting ahead. The ability to make money has become the sole determinant of one's worth.

Against this attitude Wolfe fashions his image of the natural South. If there is the tawdriness of Altamont, there is also the "Arcadian wilderness" of Pulpit Hill. This South is a land of "exquisite smell . . . clean but funky, like a big woman," of a "thousand rich odors of tree and grass and flower," "of flashing field, of wood, and hill," a land "shadowy and phantom," "opulent and seductive."[8] Wolfe's celebration of the natural South, not for what wealth it can produce but simply for what it is, recalls certain writers of the first New South, as does his denigration of the industrial impulse.

Over the mountains, at Vanderbilt University in Nashville, twelve writers and scholars were saying much the same thing.[9] Their manifesto, *I'll Take My Stand*, as Louis D. Rubin, Jr., has aptly observed, is not essentially a treatise on politics, economics, or sociology but rather "a vision of what the good life can be."[10] And the finest of all the essays is the one that most poignantly evokes that vision, John Donald Wade's moving sketch of "The Life and Death of Cousin Lucius."

Because their creators both came out of the yeoman tradition, it is no accident that Cousin Lucius in some ways strikingly resembles another Middle Georgian, Uncle Remus. Each is a teacher, each a philosophical agrarian, each skeptical of what others so blithely hail as progress. A telling passage in "Cousin Lucius" supplies a metaphoric critique of the New Order. Shortly after the turn of the century, Lucius's father has spent fifty years as superintendent of the Methodist Sunday School, and yet his flock fails to present him a gift. Twenty-five years before, when times were much harder, he had been given a silver pitcher.[11] To Wade and other figures of the Renascence, as to some writers of the first New South, the course of human experience might not be onward and upward.

In Mississippi William Faulkner was coming to a similar conclusion. Whatever the shortcomings of the Old Order, the Age of Snopes was hardly a desirable replacement. In much of Faulkner, modernism is the serpent in the garden. A scene from "The Bear" illustrates this conviction. After the annual hunt for Old Ben at long last results in his death, Ike McCaslin makes a final trip to the woods, now the property of a Memphis lumber company. He had noticed the little railroad before; the small locomotive entering the wilderness "dragging its length of train behind it . . . resembled a small dingy harmless snake vanishing into weeds." Returning, the train carried "to no destination or purpose sticks which left nowhere any scar or stump." All that has changed when Ike goes back for the last time. The lumber company is cutting on a much larger scale, building a new planing mill, and extending the spur line. "This time it was as though the train . . . had brought with it into the doomed wilderness, even before the actual axe, the shadow and portent of the new mill not even finished yet and the rails and ties which were not even laid."[12] The woods would never again be the same.

The theme continues into Southern writing since the Second World War. As Alfred Kazin has noted, the Southern writer in our time speaks against Leviathan and "for the old South as the beloved country."[13] We can see something of this in Flannery O'Connor: displaced from Poland and misplaced in the South, Mr. Guizac, a human machine, disrupts the folk society of Mrs. McIntyre's farm and ironically is killed by another machine, a tractor. We can see it in Walker Percy: diminished by mass culture, the New Southerner, in the eyes of Lancelot Lamar, is "Billy Graham on Sunday and Richard Nixon the rest of the week. He calls on Jesus and steals, he's in business, he's in politics." We can see it in James Dickey: as the weekend adventurers near their deliverance from the wild river, the first evidence they see of "civilization" is a junk-car lot.[14]

When in 1917 H. L. Mencken discovered and mapped the "Sahara of the Bozart," his cartography was rudely accurate.[15] The South was by and large artistically arid. The writers of the post-Reconstruction flowering were dead or declining, though, if Mencken's opinion of Joel Chandler Harris is any clue, he would not have thought much of them, anyway. The Sage of Baltimore could find only one native Southern writer worthy of praise, James Branch Cabell. And yet, while Mencken wrote, Ellen Glasgow had been publishing novels for twenty years, many of them good; John Gould Fletcher had recently brought out a volume of poems; and the nucleus of the Fugitive group had been meeting regularly for two years. Over the next twenty years the flood tide of the literary wave would roll in.

All this did not happen in a historical vacuum. However superior the Renascence was to postbellum writing—and it was considerably so—there were many ties binding the later period to the earlier: similar views of the role of language and form and of the uses of humor, violence, and detail of setting in fiction; even a related attitude toward the Negro, at least in its artistic rendering.[16] The greatest debt of the Renascence was to the literary opponents of the New South movement. If very few of those writers could match the talent of the better later writers, they kept alive the tradition, passed along the theme, of the South as distinctive, as, for all its faults, the beloved country, as pastoral rebuke to a grasping, misdirected mass culture. And that was no small legacy.

NOTES

INTRODUCTION

1. See Paul M. Gaston, *The New South Creed*.
2. Ibid., pp. 100, 128, 130, 139–40; George M. Fredrickson, *The Black Image in the White Mind*, pp. 210–11.
3. John Donald Wade, "Old Wine in a New Bottle," *Selected Essays and Other Writings of John Donald Wade*, p. 158; Raymond B. Nixon, *Henry W. Grady*, pp. 254–55, 340–50.
4. C. Vann Woodward, *Origins of the New South, 1877–1913*, pp. 124, 145; Gaston, *New South Creed*, pp. 68, 84.
5. Gaston, *New South Creed*, pp. 95, 99.
6. William B. Hesseltine, *Confederate Leaders in the New South*, pp. 116–25, 139; C. Vann Woodward, *Reunion and Reaction*, p. 52; C. Vann Woodward, *The South in Search of a Philosophy*, p. 3.
7. Richard H. Edmonds, *The South's Redemption*, p. 47; Gaston, *New South Creed*, pp. 98, 201–203; Woodward, *Origins of the New South*, pp. 318–19.
8. Gaston, *New South Creed*, pp. 7, 193, 198.
9. Lewis H. Blair, *The Prosperity of the South Dependent upon the Elevation of the Negro*, pp. 17–18, 21–23, 34–36.
10. Gaston, *New South Creed*, pp. 48–53; Woodward, *Origins of the New South*, p. 173.
11. Thomas Cary Johnson, *The Life and Letters of Robert Lewis Dabney*, pp. 542–43; Robert L. Dabney, "The New South," in *Discussions*, 4: 4, 17–18.
12. Robert Manson Myers, ed., *The Children of Pride*, pp. 1433–34; Charles C. Jones, Jr., *Sons of Confederate Veterans*, p. 8; Charles C. Jones, Jr., *The Old South* (1887), quoted in Claud B. Green, "Charles Colcock Jones, Jr., and Paul Hamilton Hayne," in *Georgians in Profile*, p. 257.
13. Charles C. Jones, Jr., *Georgians during the War between the States* (1889), quoted in Green, "Jones and Hayne," pp. 258–59.
14. Quoted in Woodward, *South in Search of a Philosophy*, pp. 8–9.
15. Paul H. Buck, *The Road to Reunion, 1865–1900*, pp. 221–26.
16. Quoted ibid., p. 197.
17. See Bruce Clayton, *The Savage Ideal*, p. 137.
18. For the attitude of antebellum Southern writers toward their society, see Louis D. Rubin, Jr., *The Writer in the South*, pp. 1–33; for Caruthers specifically, see John Caldwell Guilds, ed., *Nineteenth-Century Southern Fiction* (Columbus, Ohio: Charles E. Merrill, 1970), p. 95.
19. Quotation is from Woodward, *Origins of the New South*, p. 168.
20. The twelve writers analyzed herein were selected because they are among the period's most significant creative writers dealing with the New South movement. Consequently, this work does not treat Walter Hines Page, an editor and publisher much concerned with the New South movement, because he was not primarily a creative writer; nor does this work deal with Kate Chopin, an important imaginative writer, because her books do not treat the New South movement. The attitudes toward the New South movement of local colorists such as Mary Noailles Murfree, James Lane Allen, and John Fox, Jr., though not examined herein, may well deserve analysis.

CHAPTER 1

1. *New York Times*, 6 October 1881, p. 5; 7 October 1881, p. 5.
2. Ibid., 6 October 1881, p. 5; Nixon, *Grady*, pp. 189–91; Jack Blicksilver, "The International Cotton Exposition of 1881 and Its Impact upon the Economic Development of Georgia," p. 182.
3. Claude R. Flory, "Paul Hamilton Hayne and the New South," p. 391.
4. Rayburn S. Moore, *Paul Hamilton Hayne*, pp. 15–19, 33.
5. Ibid., pp. 20–21; Daniel Morley McKeithan, ed., *A Collection of Hayne Letters*, p. 219.
6. McKeithan, *Hayne Letters*, p. xv; Moore, *Hayne*, p. 167.
7. Excerpt from Wilmington (North Carolina) *Morning Star*, 11 March 1876, quoted in Charles Duffy, ed., *The Correspondence of Bayard Taylor and Paul Hamilton Hayne*, p. 24 n.
8. Hayne to Moses Coit Tyler, 26 October 1876, 20 November 1876, 16 November 1878, in McKeithan, *Hayne Letters*, pp. 360, 362, 373–74; Hayne to John Esten Cooke, 16 March 1877, ibid., p. 92; Hayne to Henry Wadsworth Longfellow, 1 April 1877, ibid., p. 150; Hayne to Susan Hayne, 28 August 1884, 4 February 1886, in William Stanley Hoole, ed., "Seven Unpublished Letters of Paul Hamilton Hayne," pp. 275, 284. The quotations are from Hoole, p. 275, and McKeithan, p. 92.
9. Hayne to Tyler, 16 May 1873, 31 December 1878, in McKeithan, *Hayne Letters*, pp. 319–20, 383; Hayne to E. C. Stedman, 8 January 1875, ibid., p. 238; Hayne to John Garland James, 15 September 1877, 14 November 1877, ibid., pp. 411, 417; Hayne to Bayard Taylor, 15 March 1876, 14 July 1877, in Duffy, *Correspondence of Taylor and Hayne*, pp. 76, 90.
10. McKeithan, *Hayne Letters*, passim; Charles Duffy, ed., "A Southern Genteelist" (April 1951), p. 68; Moore, *Hayne*, p. 110.
11. Hayne to Longfellow, 19 October 1881, in McKeithan, *Hayne Letters*, p. 178; Hayne, "The Stricken South to the North," in Paul Hamilton Hayne, *Poems*, pp. 299–300; Victor Hall Hardendorff, "Paul Hamilton Hayne and the North," pp. 168–69; Moore, *Hayne*, p. 31.
12. Flory, "Hayne and the New South," p. 391; Moore, *Hayne*, p. 128.
13. "The Exposition Ode," in Hayne, *Poems*, pp. 300–304; hereafter references to this poem shall be cited by stanza and line. Hayne retitled this poem "The Return of Peace" for the so-called complete edition, but it shall be referred to herein by its original title. The quotations are from stanza 1, lines 6 and 15, and from stanza 3, line 4.
14. "The Exposition Ode," 3. 5–10.
15. Ibid., 4. 2–4.
16. Ibid., 4. 7–8, 11–12, 14.
17. Ibid., 5. 3, 6; 7. 3, 4–5, 8–9.
18. Ibid., 9. 1–7.
19. Ibid., 10. 7–9.
20. Ibid., 11. 8.
21. Ibid., 11. 33–37.
22. Flory, "Hayne and the New South," p. 392.
23. "The Exposition Ode," 11. 31–32.
24. Ibid., 4. 17, 19.
25. Ibid., 6. 13.
26. Ibid., 11. 13–17.
27. Ibid., 5. 7–14.
28. Moore, *Hayne*, p. 128.

29. Paul Hamilton Hayne, "To the New South," in "Last Poems," Hayne Papers. The date of this poem's composition is uncertain, but available evidence indicates that it was after 1881. See John Archer Carter, "Paul Hayne's Sonnet 'To the New South,'" pp. 193–95. Ironically, the poem appeared in *Dixie*, a magazine of Southern industry, in September 1885.

30. Hayne, "To Alexander H. Stephens," in *Poems*, p. 293; Hayne to Charles Gayarré, 19 May 1885, in Charles R. Anderson, "Charles Gayarré and Paul Hamilton Hayne," p. 261; Hayne to Susan Hayne, 4 February 1886, in Hoole, "Seven Unpublished Letters," p. 284.

31. Hayne, "The Broken Battalions," in "Last Poems," Hayne Papers.

CHAPTER 2

1. John O. Beaty, *John Esten Cooke, Virginian*, pp. 1–41, passim; Mary Jo Jackson Bratton, "John Esten Cooke," p. 250.

2. Bratton, "Cooke," pp. 244, 286–88.

3. Gaston, *New South Creed*, pp. 65–68; Robert Darden Little, "The Ideology of the New South," pp. 53, 75, 93, 219–20.

4. Gaston, *New South Creed*, pp. 28–31; Little, "Ideology of the New South," pp. 57–60.

5. Beaty, *Cooke*, p. 124.

6. John Esten Cooke, *The Heir of Gaymount*, pp. 48–49, 55–56. The novel was published first serially in the *Old Guard* during 1869. Page references herein are to the publication in book form.

7. Ibid., pp. 15, 32–33, 56.

8. Ibid., pp. 50, 52.

9. Ibid., pp. 30–31, emphasis in original.

10. Jay B. Hubbell, *The South in American Literature, 1607–1900*, p. 519.

11. Quoted in Samuel Albert Link, *Pioneers of Southern Literature*, p. 268.

12. Beaty, *Cooke*, p. 128; Hubbell, *South in American Literature*, p. 519.

13. William Edward Walker, "John Esten Cooke," p. 614.

14. Quoted in Hubbell, *South in American Literature*, p. 520.

CHAPTER 3

1. See William R. Taylor, *Cavalier and Yankee: The Old South and American National Character* (1961; rpt. New York: Harper and Row, 1969).

2. Francis P. Gaines, *The Southern Plantation*, pp. 14–62, passim.

3. Ibid., p. 63.

4. Woodward, *Origins of the New South*, pp. 154–55.

5. *Boston Evening Transcript*, 13 January 1892, p. 6; Major J. B. Pond, *Eccentricities of Genius*, p. 521; Harriet R. Holman, "The Literary Career of Thomas Nelson Page, 1884–1910," p. 35.

6. Woodward, *Origins of the New South*, pp. 154–57; Gaston, *New South Creed*, pp. 159–60, 185–86.

7. Quoted in Gaston, *New South Creed*, p. 165.

8. Thomas Nelson Page, "The Old South," in *The Old South*, p. 5.

9. The quotation is from Karl Marx, *The Eighteenth Brumaire of Louis Bonaparte*, ed. C. P. Dutt (New York: International Publishers, n.d.), p. 13.

10. Holman, "Literary Career of Page," pp. 1–24, passim.

11. Ibid., pp. 12, 16.

12. Thomas Nelson Page, *In Ole Virginia; or, Marse Chan and Other Stories*. See Albion W. Tourgée, "The South as a Field for Fiction."

13. See James Kimball King, "George Washington Cable and Thomas Nelson Page," pp. 184–85; Kimball King, ed., *In Ole Virginia* by Thomas Nelson Page (Chapel Hill: University of North Carolina Press, 1969), p. xiii; Theodore L. Gross, *Thomas Nelson Page*, p. 102.

14. For treatment of the theme of reconciliation, see Buck, *Road to Reunion*, pp. 196–219.

15. "Meh Lady," in Page, *In Ole Virginia*, pp. 97–167.

16. Thomas Nelson Page, *The Negro*, pp. ix, 31–32; Fredrickson, *Black Image*, p. 260.

17. Little, "Ideology of the New South," pp. 138–39; Gaston, *New South Creed*, p. 160.

18. Holman, "Literary Career of Page," p. 75.

19. Thomas Nelson Page, *Red Rock*, esp. pp. 209, 222, 257, 269–71, 298.

20. Ibid., p. viii.

21. Benjamin W. Griffith, "Csardas at Salt Springs," pp. 54, 58.

22. Holman, "Literary Career of Page," pp. 18, 29, 37, 39.

23. Page to William Hamilton Hayne, 13 December 1887, quoted in Gross, *Page*, p. 102.

24. Little, "Ideology of the New South," p. 139; William J. Sowder, "Gerald W. Johnson, Thomas Nelson Page, and the South," p. 202; Harriet R. Holman, ed., *John Fox and Tom Page as They Were*, p. 3. Referring to the postwar resurrection of the South, Page wrote, "God in his providence had his great purpose for her and he called her forth" (*The Old South*, p. 4). Compare this with Grady's remark in 1887 that the South's "prosperity has been established by divine law" (quoted in Gaston, *New South Creed*, p. 1).

25. Thomas Nelson Page, "The Old Dominion since the War," *The Old Dominion*, p. 329.

26. Holman, "Literary Career of Page," p. 98.

27. Ibid., p. 167; Gross, *Page*, p. 123; King, "Cable and Page," pp. 296–97.

28. As evidence that Page believed the Old Order superior to the New, some commentators assert that Gordon returns to the plantation South. (See Gross, *Page*, p. 122; Holman, "Literary Career of Page," p. 167; King, "Cable and Page," pp. 296–97.) Page does not say this. When the novel ends, Gordon is working in New Leeds. His father, residing at Elphinstone, declares his intention to come and live with Gordon and his prospective bride, implying that the elder Keith will also leave the plantation. Page entitles this last chapter "The Old Ideal." Elphinstone, however, symbolizes that ideal, and Page unconsciously gives the impression that it is admirably suited for, say, a weekend retreat but that it is hardly the place for an energetic young engineer to live.

29. Holman, "Literary Career of Page," pp. 20, 88 n.; Little, "Ideology of the New South," pp. 138–39; Page, *The Old Dominion*, p. 289. Citing the work of William Gregg, an antebellum manufacturer, industrialist Daniel A. Tompkins and publicist Richard Edmonds believed with Page that the Old South had been favorably disposed to industrialism. See Little, "Ideology of the New South," p. 138; Gaston, *New South Creed*, pp. 162–64.

30. Thomas Nelson Page, *Gordon Keith*, p. 29.

31. Ibid., pp. 46–47, 51, 64, 134, 156.

32. Ibid., p. 214.

33. Ibid., p. 222.

34. Ibid.

35. Ibid., pp. 238, 271.

36. W. J. Cash, *The Mind of the South*, p. 188.

37. Gaines, *Southern Plantation*, p. 80.

38. Courtland Y. White, III, "Francis Hopkinson Smith," p. 265; Thomas Nelson Page, "Francis Hopkinson Smith," p. 307.
39. White, "Smith," p. 265.
40. Ibid., pp. 265–66.
41. Ibid., p. 266; Hubbell, *South in American Literature*, p. 730.
42. Arthur Hobson Quinn, *American Fiction*, pp. 362–68.
43. F. Hopkinson Smith, *Colonel Carter of Cartersville*, pp. 8, 10, 27.
44. Ibid., p. 61. Compare Chad's remarks with those of Sam to the narrator of "Marse Chan": "Dem wuz good ole times, marster—de bes' Sam ever see!" (Page, *In Ole Virginia*, p. 13).
45. Smith, *Colonel Carter*, p. 84.
46. Ibid., pp. 61–63.
47. Ibid., pp. 108–53, passim.
48. Ibid., pp. 130–42.
49. Ibid., pp. 20–24.
50. Ibid., p. 33.
51. Ibid., p. 10.
52. Ibid., p. 19. Smith failed to appreciate that Carter was closer to the truth here than he himself was. One need only recall the high protective tariffs and abuses in the veterans' pension system common to the period to see that Carter had a point.
53. Ibid., pp. 4, 58, 87, 100.
54. John S. Patton, "Francis Hopkinson Smith," p. 4912.
55. Smith, *Colonel Carter*, pp. 73–76, 101.
56. In 1886, Smith was among the New York audience applauding Henry Grady's address, "The New South," wherein Grady said that the region's restoration had been the result of its new attitude toward business. Nixon, *Grady*, pp. 242, 340–50.
57. Smith, *Colonel Carter*, p. 161.
58. Ibid., p. 208.
59. Allen Tate, "What Is a Traditional Society?" in *Essays of Four Decades*, p. 548.

CHAPTER 4

1. Raymond Allen Cook, *Fire from the Flint*, pp. 7, 199, et passim.
2. See, for example, ibid.; J. Zeb Wright, "Thomas Dixon"; William David Harrison, "The Thoughts of Thomas Dixon on Black and White Race Relations in American Society"; F. Garvin Davenport, Jr., *The Myth of Southern History*, pp. 23–43.
3. Davenport, *Myth of Southern History*, p. 33.
4. Ibid., pp. 34–36. See C. Hugh Holman, "A Cycle of Change in Southern Literature," p. 391.
5. Thomas Dixon, Jr., *The Leopard's Spots*, pp. 66, 71, 79, 283.
6. Thomas Dixon, Jr., *The Clansman*, pp. 66, 277.
7. Thomas Dixon, Jr., *The Traitor*, p. 331. Though the cotton-mill movement in the postwar South was motivated partly by philanthropic considerations, the profit motive was equally as important. See Woodward, *Origins of the New South*, p. 134.
8. Dixon, *Leopard's Spots*, pp. 333, 337, 362.
9. Wade, "Profits and Losses in the Life of Joel Chandler Harris," *Selected Essays*, p. 98.
10. Dixon, *The Clansman*, p. 129.

11. Cash, *Mind of the South*, pp. 157, 158.
12. Gaston, *New South Creed*, pp. 48–53.
13. John Donald Wade, "William Nathaniel Harben," p. 238.
14. Mrs. William E. Mears to Julia Mercer, 30 July 1937, quoted in Julia Mercer, "North Georgia Life in the Fiction of Will N. Harben," p. 4.
15. Wade, "Harben," p. 238; Kenneth M. Roemer, "1984 in 1894," pp. 29–42.
16. Will N. Harben, "American Backgrounds for Fiction," p. 186; see also Roemer, "1984 in 1894," p. 31 n.
17. William Dean Howells, "Mr. Harben's Georgia Fiction." See also Mercer, "North Georgia Life in Harben," pp. 119–20; and Isabella D. Harris, "The Southern Mountaineer in American Fiction, 1824–1910," pp. 177–85.
18. Robert Bush, "Will N. Harben's Northern Georgia Fiction," p. 116. Harben's reputation as a realist rests upon his accurate rendering of place and speech. His handling of romantic love, however, can only be termed mawkish even by Victorian standards. Characters, moreover, are often unrealistically typed; the most admirable ones are always middle class.
19. Will N. Harben, *Abner Daniel*, pp. 143, 285–93.
20. Peter Ketch is the triumphant trader in Longstreet's story "The Horse-Swap." See A Native Georgian [A. B. Longstreet], *Georgia Scenes, Characters, Incidents, etc., in the First Half Century of the Republic*, 2d ed. (New York: Harper and Brothers, 1850), pp. 23–31.
21. Harben, *Abner Daniel*, p. 273.
22. Ibid., p. 296.
23. Ibid., pp. 299, 300.
24. Ibid., pp. 301–302.
25. Ibid., p. 302.
26. See Woodward, *Origins of the New South*, pp. 120–21, 187, 292–95, 312; and John F. Stover, *The Railroads of the South, 1865–1900: A Study in Finance and Control* (Chapel Hill: University of North Carolina Press, 1955), p. 279.
27. Harben, *Abner Daniel*, p. 297; emphasis in original.
28. Ibid., p. 295.
29. In addition to *Abner Daniel*, see the following novels by Harben: *Pole Baker*; *Ann Boyd*; *Gilbert Neal*; *Dixie Hart*.
30. Harben, *Ann Boyd*, p. 122.
31. Ibid., p. 296.
32. Ibid., p. 279 et passim.
33. Harben, *Dixie Hart*, pp. 284–93; quotation is from p. 292.
34. Ibid., p. 284.
35. Will N. Harben, *The Georgians*, pp. 38, 212.
36. See ibid., pp. 129–32.
37. See Harben, *Abner Daniel*, pp. 75–76.
38. See Harben, *Gilbert Neal*, pp. 32, 84.
39. Harben, *The Georgians*, p. 81.

CHAPTER 5

1. Aubrey Harrison Starke, *Sidney Lanier*, pp. 5–37, passim.
2. Ibid., pp. 44–45, 62, 67–68.
3. Ibid., pp. 70, 72, 74, 111–12.
4. Sidney Lanier to Bayard Taylor, 7 August 1875, in *The Centennial Edition of the Works of Sidney Lanier*, 9: 230; hereafter cited as Lanier, *Works*.
5. Lanier, *Works*, 5: 5–193, passim. *Tiger-Lilies* was published originally by Hurd and Houghton, New York.

6. "John Lockwood's Mill," in Lanier, *Works*, 5: 231–46. This fragment was unpublished until 1945 when it appeared in the *Works*.

7. The setting is surmised from evidence within the fragment.

8. In this regard, see Woodward, *Reunion and Reaction*, p. 57, and *Origins of the New South*, pp. 4–21, passim.

9. Lanier, *Works*, 5: 238.

10. Ibid.

11. Ibid., p. 243; emphasis in original. Meta fails to note that the English became lords of the sea through their response to the commercial impulse.

12. Ibid., p. 231.

13. Ibid., p. 232.

14. Ibid., esp. pp. 232–33.

15. See Lanier to Charles Day, 29 April 1869, and Lanier to Robert Sampson Lanier, 4 May 1869, 10 May 1869, in *Works*, 8: 18, 21, 26.

16. "Thar's More in the Man Than Thar Is in the Land," in Lanier, *Works*, 1: 22–23; subsequent quotations from poems are cited by stanza and line. This piece was published first in the Macon *Telegraph and Messenger*, 7 February 1871.

17. Lanier, "Thar's More in the Man," 1. 3–4.

18. Ibid., 10. 5–6; emphasis in original.

19. "Jones's Private Argument," in Lanier, *Works*, 1: 24–25. This poem appeared first in *Southern Farm and Home* 2 (July 1871): 338.

20. Lanier, "Jones's Private Argument," 3. 2–5; emphasis in original.

21. "9 from 8," in Lanier, *Works* 1: 194–96. This poem was first published in *Independent* 36 (13 March 1884): 321, nearly three years after Lanier's death.

22. Lanier, "9 from 8," 3. 10–11.

23. Ibid., 1. 14–15; 2. 14–15; 3. 14–15; 4. 14–15.

24. "The Homestead," in Lanier, *Works*, 1: 25–28, published first in *Southern Farm and Home* 2 (August 1871): 392.

25. Lanier, "The Homestead," 3. 1–2.

26. Jack De Bellis, *Sidney Lanier*, p. 61; Starke, *Lanier*, pp. 156–59, 167–69.

27. "Corn," in Lanier, *Works*, 1: 34–39.

28. Lanier, "Corn," 5. 1, 6.

29. Ibid., 5. 7.

30. Ibid., 9. 5–6.

31. Ibid., 11. 4–5.

32. Ibid., 11. 16–17, 36–40.

33. Ibid., 12. 11–12, 16.

34. De Bellis, *Lanier*, p. 66.

35. "The Hard Times in Elfland," in Lanier, *Works*, 1: 105–11, published first in Baltimore *Every Saturday*, 22 December 1877. Starke, *Lanier*, p. 290, favors an allegorical reading of this poem, and considering Lanier's concern for the South shown in some of his previous poetic works, one may readily agree with Starke's interpretation. Lanier may have felt that "Hard Times in Elfland" might have an impact on the allegorical level upon the parents who read the poem to their children.

36. "The Symphony," in Lanier, *Works*, 1: 46–56, published first in *Lippincott's Magazine* 15 (June 1875): 677–84.

37. "The Marshes of Glynn," in Lanier, *Works*, 1: 119–22, published first (anonymously) in *A Masque of Poets* (Boston: Roberts Brothers, 1878), pp. 88–94.

38. "Sunrise," in Lanier, *Works*, 1: 144–49, published first in *Independent* 34 (14 December 1882): 1. Quoted passage is from verse paragraph 13, lines 1–6.

39. Louis D. Rubin, Jr., "The Passion of Sidney Lanier," *William Elliott Shoots a Bear*, pp. 134, 138; Little, "Ideology of the New South," pp. 143–44.

40. "The New South," in Lanier, *Works*, 5: 334–58; quotation is from pp. 334, 338. This essay appeared first in *Scribner's Monthly* 20 (October 1880): 840–51, less than a year before Lanier died; emphasis in original.

41. "The New South," in Lanier, *Works*, 5: 358.

42. In this connection, see Little, "Ideology of the New South," pp. 143–44.

43. See Rubin, "The Passion of Lanier," pp. 107–44.

44. When Aubrey Starke's biography of Lanier posited a direct line between him and the Agrarians, those among them who had made up the older group of Fugitive poets, especially Robert Penn Warren and Allen Tate, hastened to deny it. They agreed with Edwin Mims's older assessment (*Sidney Lanier*) of Lanier as a New South writer, basing their opinion, as did Mims, primarily on Lanier's gradually developing conciliatory attitude toward the North in political matters. One is tempted to say that their low regard of Lanier's talents as a poet prompted them in part to disavow any ideological connection with him. See Allen Tate, "A Southern Romantic," pp. 67–68; and Robert Penn Warren, "The Blind Poet." Starke responded to Warren and Tate in "The Agrarians Deny a Leader," an article followed immediately by John Crowe Ransom's "Hearts and Heads," which attempted to adjudicate the dispute.

45. Andrew Nelson Lytle, "The Hind Tit," in Twelve Southerners, *I'll Take My Stand*, p. 205.

CHAPTER 6

1. Gaines, *Southern Plantation*, p. 74.

2. Louis D. Rubin, Jr., "Joel Chandler Harris," in Richard Beale Davis, C. Hugh Holman, and Louis D. Rubin, Jr., eds., *Southern Writing, 1585–1920*, p. 641; Paul M. Cousins, *Joel Chandler Harris*, pp. 3, 22.

3. Joel Chandler Harris, *Gabriel Tolliver*, p. 95.

4. Cousins, *Harris*, pp. 34, 61.

5. Ibid., pp. 68–92, passim.

6. Ibid., pp. 97–98.

7. Woodward, *South in Search of a Philosophy*, p. 7; Rubin, *Writer in the South*, pp. 11–12. See also Louis D. Rubin, Jr., "Uncle Remus and the Ubiquitous Rabbit," *William Elliott Shoots a Bear*, p. 83.

8. For a picture of Harris's personality, see Cousins, *Harris*, p. 214; Herbert F. Smith, "Joel Chandler Harris's Contributions to *Scribner's Monthly* and *Century Magazine*, 1880–1887," p. 171; and Harris to William Malone Baskervill, 18 March 1895, 15 April 1895, in Harris, "Letters of Uncle Remus," pp. 219, 221.

· 9. Wade, "Profits and Losses in the Life of Joel Chandler Harris," *Selected Essays*, p. 100.

10. In 1886, Grady told a Northern audience, "No section shows a more prosperous laboring population than the negroes of the South" (Nixon, *Grady*, p. 346). Harris knew better.

11. "Ananias," in Joel Chandler Harris, *Balaam and His Master and Other Sketches and Stories*, pp. 113–48.

12. "Blue Dave," in Joel Chandler Harris, *Mingo and Other Sketches in Black and White*, pp. 164–228.

13. Joel Chandler Harris, *The Bishop and the Boogerman*.

14. "The Old Bascom Place," in Harris, *Balaam and His Master*, pp. 192–293.

15. "Free Joe and the Rest of the World," in Joel Chandler Harris, *Free Joe and Other Georgian Sketches*, pp. 3–29.

16. Joel Chandler Harris, *The Complete Tales of Uncle Remus*, pp. xxv, 358, 459, 701. See also Louis D. Rubin, Jr., "Southern Local Color and the Black Man," pp. 1017–18.

17. See "Uncle Remus with the Toothache," in Joel Chandler Harris, *Uncle Remus*, p. 231.

18. "The Emigrants," ibid., pp. 242–44.

19. Harris, *Gabriel Tolliver*, p. 114.

20. Cousins, *Harris*, p. 223.

21. "Turnip Salad as a Text" and "Race Improvement," in Harris, *Uncle Remus*, pp. 228, 236.

22. Joel Chandler Harris, "How Education Will Solve the So-called Negro Problem," New York *Journal*, 3 November 1901, reprinted in Julia Collier Harris, *The Life and Letters of Joel Chandler Harris*, pp. 500–503. See also Jerry Allen Herndon, "Social Comment in the Writings of Joel Chandler Harris," p. 95; and Fredrickson, *Black Image*, pp. 204–16, passim.

23. "How Education Will Solve the So-called Negro Problem," in Julia Harris, *Life and Letters*, p. 502. See also Rubin, "Uncle Remus," p. 100.

24. Harris, *Gabriel Tolliver*, p. 189; Joel Chandler Harris, *The Chronicles of Aunt Minervy Ann*.

25. Quoted in Fredrickson, *Black Image*, p. 215.

26. Harris, *Gabriel Tolliver*, p. 36.

27. "Miss Puss's Parasol," in Joel Chandler Harris, *The Making of a Statesman and Other Stories*, p. 218.

28. See Joel Chandler Harris, *Told by Uncle Remus*, pp. 59, 89–90, 289.

29. "At Teague Poteet's," in Harris, *Mingo*, pp. 34–163.

30. "Trouble on Lost Mountain," in Harris, *Free Joe*, pp. 133–82.

31. "Azalia," ibid., pp. 183–312. Quotations are from pp. 206–207, 212.

32. "Aunt Fountain's Prisoner," ibid., pp. 98–132.

33. Ibid., p. 107.

34. "The Old Bascom Place," in Harris, *Balaam and His Master*, pp. 192–293.

35. "Azalia," in Harris, *Free Joe*, p. 311; Harris, *Complete Remus*, p. 579. For a variant view of Harris's attitude toward cities and the process of urbanization, see Herndon, "Social Comment in Harris," p. 156.

36. "The Baby's Christmas," in Joel Chandler Harris, *Tales of the Home Folks in Peace and War*," pp. 377–417. Quotation is from p. 397.

37. Harris, *Complete Remus*, p. 826.

38. "Brother Rabbit's Cradle," ibid., pp. 671–79.

39. "Brother Fox Follows the Fashion," ibid., pp. 647–53.

40. "How Old Craney-Crow Lost His Head," ibid., pp. 640–47.

41. Ibid., pp. 339, 545, 598, 701, 772.

42. When Harris complimented the Georgia town of Harmony Grove by writing that its residents were "not trying to get rich in a day" ("Mr. Sanders to a Boston Capitalist," p. 196), a citizen of the town objected. Rather than a "'Sleepy Hollow,' or . . . little cross-roads town with no get-up-and-get," the correspondent wrote, Harmony Grove "is to-day the best town of its size in Georgia" (quoted in Julia Harris, *Life and Letters*, p. 433). The boomers must have been in the majority, for Harmony Grove was shortly thereafter renamed Commerce. See Allen D. Candler and Clement A. Evans, eds., *Georgia: Comprising Sketches of Counties, Towns, Events, Institutions, and Persons, Arranged in Cyclopedic Form* (Atlanta: State Historical Association, 1906), 1: 434.

43. Harris, *Gabriel Tolliver*, pp. 18, 110–11.

44. Harris, *Making of a Statesman*, p. 15.

45. Harris, *Complete Remus*, p. 826.

46. Harris, *Gabriel Tolliver*, pp. 404, 433. Harris's champions of constitutional liberty bear a marked resemblance to those men C. Vann Woodward called Redeemers. Woodward, *Origins of the New South*, pp. 1–22.

47. *Joel Chandler Harris, Editor and Essayist*, p. 194.
48. Harris, "Mr. Sanders," p. 198.
49. Ibid.
50. Ibid., p. 196.
51. Ibid., p. 199.
52. Quoted in *Joel Chandler Harris, Editor and Essayist*, p. 386.
53. Ibid.
54. Joel Chandler Harris, "Progress—in the Best and Highest Sense," p. 7.
55. Ibid., pp. 7–8.

CHAPTER 7

1. Arlin Turner, "Mark Twain and the South," p. 495; Charles Neider, ed., *The Adventures of Colonel Sellers*, p. xvii, quoting Mark Twain's preface to the London edition of *The Gilded Age*. *The Adventures of Colonel Sellers* is Mark Twain's part of *The Gilded Age*. "Old Times on the Mississippi" is roughly the first half of *Life on the Mississippi*, published first serially in 1875 in the *Atlantic Monthly*.
2. Neider, *Adventures of Colonel Sellers*, p. xx; Henry Nash Smith, *Mark Twain*, p. 76; Justin Kaplan, *Mr. Clemens and Mark Twain*, p. 121.
3. H. Wayne Morgan, *American Writers in Rebellion*, p. 2; V. L. Parrington, *Main Currents in American Thought* (New York: Harcourt, Brace and Company, 1930), 3: 88.
4. William Dean Howells, *My Mark Twain*, pp. 20–21. *Colonel Sellers*, adapted from *The Gilded Age* and produced first in 1874, was quite popular during the midseventies and was revived regularly until 1888. See Bryant Morey French, *Mark Twain and "The Gilded Age,"* p. 242.
5. Kaplan, *Mr. Clemens and Mark Twain*, pp. 85, 256–57, 282; Arthur G. Pettit, *Mark Twain and the South*, p. 189.
6. Kaplan, *Mr. Clemens and Mark Twain*, pp. 282, 298; Justin Kaplan, ed., *Mark Twain*, p. xvi.
7. Kaplan, *Mr. Clemens and Mark Twain*, p. 96.
8. Woodward, *Origins of the New South*, pp. 67–72; Gaston, *New South Creed*, p. 7. In recent years, attempts have been made to revise the Woodward view of the political leaders of the post-Reconstruction South. See James Tice Moore, "Redeemers Reconsidered: Change and Continuity in the Democratic South, 1870–1900," *Journal of Southern History* 44 (August 1978): 357–78, an arresting, if unconvincing, article.
9. Woodward, *Reunion and Reaction*, pp. 55, 80, 85, 89–90.
10. Ibid., p. 56; Woodward, *South in Search of a Philosophy*, p. 3; Gaston, *New South Creed*, pp. 7, 41, 69.
11. Woodward, *Reunion and Reaction*, p. 57.
12. Mark Twain and Charles Dudley Warner, *The Gilded Age*, pp. 134–35, 186–87.
13. Quoted in Gaston, *New South Creed*, pp. 1, 24.
14. Woodward, *Reunion and Reaction*, pp. 53–54.
15. Ibid., pp. 52, 55, 86.
16. Mark Twain, *The Gilded Age*, pp. 264, 272–73.
17. Gaston, *New South Creed*, pp. 117–50; Fredrickson, *Black Image*, pp. 198–227.
18. Mark Twain, *The Gilded Age*, pp. 274, 311.
19. Ibid., pp. 142–43, 222, 245, 295. By 1873, Mark Twain had modified his earlier anti-Negro prejudices. He was still no egalitarian on the race issue, how-

ever, and protection of the political rights of black men ranked lower among his priorities than elimination of official corruption. For his changing attitude toward the Negro early in his career, see a series of articles by Arthur G. Pettit: "Mark Twain, Unreconstructed Southerner, and His View of the Negro, 1835–1860"; "Mark Twain's Attitude toward the Negro in the West, 1861–1867"; "Mark Twain and the Negro, 1867–1869." See also Pettit, *Mark Twain and the South*, in which a major theme is Mark Twain's views of the black man.

20. Arlin Turner, "James Lampton, Mark Twain's Model for Colonel Sellers," pp. 593–94.

21. Quoted in French, *Mark Twain and "The Gilded Age,"* p. 169.

22. Mark Twain, *Life on the Mississippi*, pp. 334, 375.

23. Ibid., pp. 328, 333, 341.

24. Mark Twain, *A Connecticut Yankee at King Arthur's Court*, p. 36.

25. See Robert Penn Warren, "Mark Twain," pp. 485–87; and Rubin, *Writer in the South*, pp. 71–74.

26. Grady, "The New South," in Nixon, *Grady*, p. 348.

27. Mark Twain, *Connecticut Yankee*, pp. 252–352, passim.

28. Ibid., p. 352; emphasis in original.

29. Henry Nash Smith, *Mark Twain's Fable of Progress*, p. 93.

30. Ibid., p. 54.

31. Ibid., p. 47.

32. Mark Twain, *Connecticut Yankee*, p. 103.

33. Smith, *Mark Twain's Fable*, p. 95.

34. Mark Twain, *Connecticut Yankee*, p. 409.

35. Smith, *Mark Twain's Fable*, pp. 40–41.

36. Smith, *Mark Twain*, pp. 74–75; Dixon Wecter, *Sam Clemens of Hannibal*, p. 65.

CHAPTER 8

1. Edward King, *The Great South*, p. xxxv.

2. For Cable's first thirty years, see Arlin Turner, *George W. Cable*, pp. 3–51.

3. Cable's *Old Creole Days*, published in 1879, contains two stories, "Belles Demoiselles Plantation" and "'Tite Poulette," that broach this subject.

4. See "My Politics," in George W. Cable, *The Negro Question*, p. 15. "My Politics" was unpublished until Arlin Turner, the editor, included it in this volume.

5. Little, "Ideology of the New South," pp. 151–52.

6. "The Good Samaritan," in Cable, *The Negro Question*, pp. 37–38.

7. George W. Cable, *"The Silent South," Together with "The Freedman's Case in Equity" and "The Convict Lease System,"* pp. 115–82.

8. "The Freedman's Case in Equity," in Cable, *Silent South*, pp. 1–39.

9. Ibid., p. 34. The phrase "a fool's dream" occurs in Cable's essay "The Silent South," ibid., p. 54, but is equally applicable in the context of "The Freedman's Case."

10. "The Freedman's Case," ibid., p. 35.

11. Turner, *Cable*, pp. 198, 218.

12. Hayne to Julia C. R. Dorr, 30 August 1884, in Duffy, "A Southern Genteelist," p. 22; Hayne to Charles Gayarré, 27 January 1885, 19 May 1885, in Anderson, "Gayarré and Hayne," pp. 227, 247.

13. Gayarré to Paul Hamilton Hayne, 30 January 1885, in Anderson, "Gayarré and Hayne," p. 228.

14. Henry W. Grady, "In Plain Black and White."
15. Turner, *Cable*, p. 223.
16. "The Southern Struggle for Pure Government," in Cable, *The Negro Question*, p. 271.
17. Philip Butcher, *George W. Cable*, pp. 137, 253.
18. George W. Cable, *The Grandissimes*, p. 43.
19. Quoted in Louis D. Rubin, Jr., *George W. Cable*, pp. 87–88 n; emphasis in original.
20. George W. Cable, *Dr. Sevier*, p. 118.
21. Ibid., p. 7.
22. Ibid., p. 149.
23. Ibid., p. 250.
24. "The Convict Lease System in the Southern States," in Cable, *Silent South*, pp. 115–82.
25. "My Politics," in Cable, *The Negro Question*, p. 21.
26. "Southern Struggle for Pure Government," ibid., p. 252.
27. Ibid., pp. 252–53.
28. Turner, *Cable*, p. 290. See two essays by Louis D. Rubin, Jr.: "The Road to Yoknapatawpha," in his *Writers of the Modern South*, pp. 21–42; and "Politics and the Novel," in his *William Elliott Shoots a Bear*, pp. 61–81.
29. Turner, *Cable*, p. 291.
30. George W. Cable, *John March, Southerner*, p. 139.
31. Ibid.
32. Ibid., p. 483.
33. Ibid., p. 95.
34. Ibid., pp. 120–22.
35. Ibid., p. 141.
36. See Rubin, *Cable*, p. 230.
37. Cable, *The Grandissimes*, p. 193.
38. Cable, *Dr. Sevier*, p. 471; Cable, *John March*, p. 327. In *Dr. Sevier* the remark is an authorial comment; in *John March* it is made by a sympathetically portrayed character.

CHAPTER 9

1. Charles W. Chesnutt to H. D. Robins, 27 September 1900, in Helen M. Chesnutt, *Charles Waddell Chesnutt*, p. 152.
2. Julian D. Mason, Jr., "Charles W. Chesnutt as Southern Author," p. 89.
3. H. Chesnutt, *Chesnutt*, p. 4.
4. Ibid., pp. 5–6, 8–9, 15–16.
5. Quoted in Sylvia Lyons Render, "Eagle with Clipped Wings," p. 15 n.
6. Quoted in H. Chesnutt, *Chesnutt*, pp. 13, 21. J. Noel Heermance, in *Charles W. Chesnutt*, p. 68, states that Chesnutt "never seriously considered" passing. Darwin Turner, however, in his introduction to Chesnutt's novel *The House behind the Cedars*, p. x, maintains that Chesnutt "seriously considered" passing. That Chesnutt conceived the idea at all shows he was dissatisfied with his lot. The theme of passing, moreover, occurs often in his fiction.
7. Quoted in H. Chesnutt, *Chesnutt*, p. 21.
8. See Charles W. Chesnutt, "Tobe's Tribulations," p. 658; and Charles W. Chesnutt, "Post-Bellum–Pre-Harlem," in *Breaking into Print*, p. 51.
9. See the following stories by Chesnutt: "Po' Sandy," in Charles W. Chesnutt, *The Conjure Woman*, pp. 36–63; "Dave's Neckliss," in Davis, Holman, and Rubin,

Southern Writing, pp. 879–88; "Mars Jeems's Nightmare," in *The Conjure Woman*, pp. 64–102; "A Victim of Heredity; or, Why the Darkey Loves Chicken"; "The Gray Wolf's Ha'nt," in *The Conjure Woman*, pp. 162–94. I should like to thank Professor William L. Andrews for sharing with me his bibliography of Chesnutt's stories and for permitting me to reproduce copies of obscure stories in his possession.

10. Chesnutt, "Dave's Neckliss," p. 880.

11. Charles W. Chesnutt, "Aunt Mimy's Son."

12. Charles W. Chesnutt, "A Roman Antique."

13. "Sis Becky's Pickaninny," in Chesnutt, *The Conjure Woman*, p. 159. These words are spoken by Miss Annie, the white narrator's wife and a woman of great sensitivity, whom Chesnutt uses to comment upon the South's racial arrangement.

14. Charles W. Chesnutt, "Uncle Peter's House."

15. "The Web of Circumstance," in Charles W. Chesnutt, *The Wife of His Youth and Other Stories of the Color Line*, pp. 291–323.

16. See Charles W. Chesnutt, "The March of Progress." Chesnutt objected to the doctrine of race solidarity, preferring that the Negro be assimilated into American society. For this to occur, Chesnutt believed that, contrary to the ideas of Booker Washington who placed first emphasis on Negro economic improvement, white men must live up to democratic ideals. See August Meier, *Negro Thought in America, 1880–1915*, p. 243.

17. Charles W. Chesnutt, "The Disfranchisement of the Negro," in *The Negro Problem*, p. 102; Render, "Eagle with Clipped Wings," pp. 348–49.

18. "The Bouquet," in Chesnutt, *Wife of His Youth*, p. 270.

19. Between Chesnutt's two volumes of stories and *The Colonel's Dream*, he published two novels: *The House behind the Cedars* (1900), a story of interracial love; and *The Marrow of Tradition* (1901), a fictional rendering of the Wilmington, North Carolina, race riot of 1898.

20. Charles W. Chesnutt, *The Colonel's Dream*, p. 197.

21. Two such men are Archibald Straight in *The House behind the Cedars* and John Delamere in *The Marrow of Tradition*.

22. The lazy South is a peripheral theme in much of Chesnutt's work. See also "Mars Jeems's Nightmare," in *The Conjure Woman*, p. 68; "Uncle Peter's House," passim.; "The Sheriff's Children," in *Wife of His Youth*, p. 62; "McDugald's Mule."

23. Chesnutt, *The Colonel's Dream*, p. 16.

24. Ibid., pp. 108, 109.

25. In this regard Chesnutt is countering the ideal of the leisurely South as a land where materialism has no place and where ease is a way of life. The implication is that indolence and leisure are not the same. See David Bertelson, *The Lazy South*, esp. pp. 237–46.

26. William L. Andrews, "The Fiction of Charles W. Chesnutt," pp. 219–50, passim, argues that Fetters is too evil to be credible. It may be, however, that Chesnutt was unconcerned with Fetters as a character. The reader seldom encounters him directly. He is rather a dark presence that, Snopes-like, symbolizes the ills of the New South.

27. Cash, *Mind of the South*, p. 137.

28. Chesnutt, *The Colonel's Dream*, p. 265.

29. Ibid., p. 72.

30. Ibid., p. 283.

31. Ibid., p. 280.

32. See Chesnutt, "Disfranchisement of the Negro," passim.
33. Chesnutt, *The Colonel's Dream*, p. 46.
34. David D. Britt, "Chesnutt's Conjure Tales," p. 277.

CHAPTER 10

1. [Walter Hines Page], *The Southerner: A Novel, Being the Autobiography of Nicholas Worth* (New York: Doubleday, Page and Company, 1909). This novel ran serially in the *Atlantic Monthly* in 1906.
2. Richard M. Weaver, *The Southern Tradition at Bay*, pp. 315–21; John Fox, Jr., *The Trail of the Lonesome Pine* (1908; rpt. New York: Charles Scribner's Sons, 1917); John Fox, Jr., to Thomas Nelson Page, 22 April 1895, in Holman, *Fox and Page*, p. 24.
3. Ellen Glasgow, *A Certain Measure*, p. 13; Ellen Glasgow, *The Woman Within*, pp. 97, 98.
4. See the following novels by Ellen Glasgow: *The Voice of the People*; *The Deliverance*; *The Ancient Law*; *The Romance of a Plain Man*; *The Miller of Old Church*; *Virginia*.
5. E. Stanly Godbold, Jr., *Ellen Glasgow and the Woman Within*, pp. 36–37.
6. Ibid., pp. 27–28. For a convenient chronology of Miss Glasgow's life, see Blair Rouse, *Ellen Glasgow*, pp. 11–13.
7. Rouse, *Glasgow*, pp. 28–29; J. R. Raper, *Without Shelter*, p. 42; Glasgow, *Certain Measure*, p. 118.
8. Rouse, *Glasgow*, pp. 11–12.
9. By the time Ellen Glasgow reached forty, she was almost deaf, and death had taken her mother, a brother, a sister, a brother-in-law, and her lover. See ibid.
10. Glasgow, *Certain Measure*, pp. 12, 82; Ellen Glasgow to Frank Morley, 7 December 1943, in *Letters of Ellen Glasgow*, p. 340.
11. See Glasgow, *Certain Measure*, p. 4.
12. Ibid., p. 76.
13. Louis D. Rubin, Jr., "Two in Richmond," pp. 116, 139; Allen W. Moger, *Virginia*, p. 129.
14. See Daniel Watkins Patterson, "Ellen Glasgow's Use of Virginia History," pp. 57–60; and Richard H. W. Dillard, "Pragmatic Realism," p. 118.
15. Glasgow, *Romance of a Plain Man*, pp. 240, 273.
16. Ibid., pp. 28, 178.
17. Ibid., p. 294. General Bolingbroke's imagery calls to mind the remarks in 1889 of Alabama ironmaster Henry Fairchild De Bardeleben on his business practices. "I was the eagle," he said, "and I wanted to eat up all the craw-fish I could,—swallow up all the little fellows, and I did it." De Bardeleben, though, was later swallowed by John H. Inman, Tennessee industrialist, who himself was subsequently swallowed by J. P. Morgan, "the biggest eagle of them all." See Woodward, *Origins of the New South*, pp. 128–29. In *Virginia*, Glasgow again compared a railroad with a serpent (p. 81).
18. Glasgow, *Romance of a Plain Man*, p. 410.
19. Ibid., p. 28.
20. Ibid., p. 295.
21. Ibid., p. 214.
22. Ibid., p. 291.
23. Ibid., p. 363.
24. See Frederick P. W. McDowell, *Ellen Glasgow and the Ironic Art of Fiction*, p.

91; Louis Auchincloss, *Ellen Glasgow*, pp. 18–19; Joan Foster Santas, *Ellen Glasgow's American Dream*, pp. 124–25; Frederick P. W. McDowell, "The Prewar Novels," p. 83.

25. Quotation is from Woodward, *Origins of the New South*, p. 436.
26. Moger, *Virginia*, p. 131.
27. Quoted in ibid., p. 129.
28. McDowell, "Prewar Novels," p. 105.
29. Glasgow, *Virginia*, pp. 163, 165, 362.
30. Ibid., pp. 12, 18.
31. Ibid., p. 24.
32. Ibid., p. 65.
33. Nevertheless, Glasgow uses Gabriel to make a penetrating observation of the Negro, a subject largely neglected in her work. Gabriel has the humility and the good sense to feel that white people really do not know black people. Such an attitude contrasts refreshingly with that of those white Southerners who arrogantly believed they understood the Negro better than anyone else did; see ibid., p. 375.
34. Marion K. Richards, *Ellen Glasgow's Development as a Novelist*, p. 127; Rubin, "Two in Richmond," p. 122. See also Ellen Glasgow to Allen Tate, 3 April 1933, *Letters*, p. 134.
35. Glasgow, *Certain Measure*, pp. 145, 255; Stark Young to Donald Davidson, 25 July 1930, in *Stark Young: A Life in the Arts: Letters, 1900–1962*, 2 vols., ed. John Pilkington (Baton Rouge: Louisiana State University Press, 1975), 1: 341.

EPILOGUE

1. David M. Potter, "The Enigma of the South," *The South and the Sectional Conflict* (Baton Rouge: Louisiana State University Press, 1968), p. 16.
2. See above, chap. 6, n. 42.
3. See George B. Tindall, *The Persistent Tradition in New South Politics*, p. 60.
4. George B. Tindall, *The Emergence of the New South, 1913–1945*, pp. 70–110; quotation is from p. 110.
5. Quoted in ibid., pp. 104, 110.
6. C. Hugh Holman, "The Dark, Ruined Helen of His Blood: Thomas Wolfe and the South," in *The Roots of Southern Writing: Essays on the Literature of the American South* (Athens: University of Georgia Press, 1972), p. 129.
7. Thomas Wolfe, *Look Homeward, Angel* (1929; rpt. New York: Bantam Books, 1970), pp. 232, 343, 545.
8. Ibid., pp. 78, 147, 542, 543.
9. On the ideological similarity between Wolfe and the Agrarians, see Holman, "The Dark, Ruined Helen," pp. 128–29.
10. Twelve Southerners, *I'll Take My Stand*, p. xv.
11. Ibid., p. 287.
12. William Faulkner, "The Bear," in *The Portable Faulkner*, ed. Malcolm Cowley, rev. ed. (New York: Viking Press, 1968), pp. 309–11.
13. Alfred Kazin, *Bright Book of Life: American Novelists and Storytellers from Hemingway to Mailer* (Boston: Little, Brown and Company, 1973), p. 41.
14. Flannery O'Connor, "The Displaced Person," in *3 by Flannery O'Connor* (New York: New American Library, n.d.), pp. 262–99; Walker Percy, *Lancelot* (New York: Farrar, Straus and Giroux, 1977), p. 220. Although the scene by James Dickey does not occur in his novel *Deliverance*, it does in the film *Deliverance* (1972), for which Dickey wrote the screenplay. For a different view of Dickey

and Percy, see Jack Temple Kirby, *Media-Made Dixie: The South in the American Imagination* (Baton Rouge: Louisiana State University Press, 1978), pp. 160–61, 164–65.

15. H. L. Mencken, "The Sahara of the Bozart," in Davis, Holman, and Rubin, *Southern Writing*, pp. 971–79.

16. For a good essay on the postbellum-Renascence connection, see "Postscript: The Southern Literary Renascence," ibid., pp. 980–87.

SELECT BIBLIOGRAPHY

I. GENERAL WORKS

Bertelson, David. *The Lazy South*. New York: Oxford University Press, 1967.

Blair, Lewis H. *A Southern Prophecy: The Prosperity of the South Dependent upon the Elevation of the Negro*. 1889. Edited by C. Vann Woodward. Boston: Little, Brown and Company, 1964.

Blicksilver, Jack. "The International Cotton Exposition of 1881 and Its Impact upon the Economic Development of Georgia." *Cotton History Review* 1 (October 1960): 175–94.

Buck, Paul H. *The Road to Reunion, 1865–1900*. Boston: Little, Brown and Company, 1937.

Cash, W. J. *The Mind of the South*. 1941. Reprint. New York: Vintage Books, n.d.

Clayton, Bruce. *The Savage Ideal: Intolerance and Intellectual Leadership in the South, 1890–1914*. Baltimore: Johns Hopkins University Press, 1972.

Dabney, Robert L. "The New South." *Discussions*, vol. 4. Edited by C. R. Vaughan. Mexico, Mo.: Crescent Book House, 1897.

Davis, Richard Beale; Holman, C. Hugh; and Rubin, Louis D., Jr., eds. *Southern Writing, 1585–1920*. New York: Odyssey Press, 1970.

Edmonds, Richard H. *The South's Redemption: From Poverty to Prosperity*. Baltimore: Manufacturers' Record Company, 1890.

Fredrickson, George M. *The Black Image in the White Mind: The Debate on Afro-American Character and Destiny, 1817–1914*. New York: Harper and Row, 1971.

Gaines, Francis P. *The Southern Plantation: A Study in the Development and the Accuracy of a Tradition*. New York: Columbia University Press, 1924.

Gaston, Paul M. *The New South Creed: A Study in Southern Mythmaking*. New York: Alfred A. Knopf, 1970.

Grady, Henry W. "In Plain Black and White: A Reply to Mr. Cable." *Century Magazine* 29 (April 1885): 909–17.

_____. "The New South." In *Henry W. Grady: Spokesman of the New South* by Raymond B. Nixon. New York: Alfred A. Knopf, 1943.

Hesseltine, William B. *Confederate Leaders in the New South*. Baton Rouge: Louisiana State University Press, 1950.

Holman, C. Hugh. "A Cycle of Change in Southern Literature." In *The South in Continuity and Change*, edited by John C. McKinney and Edgar T. Thompson. Durham: Duke University Press, 1965.

Hubbell, Jay B. *The South in American Literature, 1607–1900*. Durham: Duke University Press, 1954.

Johnson, Thomas Cary. *The Life and Letters of Robert Lewis Dabney*. Richmond: Presbyterian Committee of Publication, 1903.

Jones, Charles C., Jr. *Sons of Confederate Veterans*. Augusta, Ga.: Chronicle Publishing Company, 1891.

King, Edward. *The Great South*. 1875. Edited by W. Magruder Drake and Robert R. Jones. Reprint. Baton Rouge: Louisiana State University Press, 1972.

Little, Robert Darden. "The Ideology of the New South: A Study in the Development of Ideas, 1865–1910." Ph.D. dissertation, University of Chicago, 1950.

Myers, Robert Manson, ed. *The Children of Pride: A True Story of Georgia and the Civil War*. New Haven: Yale University Press, 1972.

Nixon, Raymond B. *Henry W. Grady: Spokesman of the New South*. New York: Alfred A. Knopf, 1943.

Osterweis, Rollin G. *The Myth of the Lost Cause, 1865–1900*. Hamden, Conn.: Archon Books, 1973.

Rubin, Louis D., Jr. "Southern Local Color and the Black Man." *Southern Review* 6 (October 1970): 1011–30.

_____. *The Writer in the South: Studies in a Literary Community*. Athens: University of Georgia Press, 1972.

Tate, Allen. "What Is a Traditional Society?" *Essays of Four Decades*. Chicago: The Swallow Press, 1968.

Tindall, George B. "Beyond the Mainstream: The Ethnic Southerners." *Journal of Southern History* 40 (February 1974): 3–18.

_____. *The Emergence of the New South, 1913–1945. A History of the South*, edited by Wendell Holmes Stephenson and E. Merton Coulter, vol. 10. Baton Rouge: Louisiana State University Press, 1967.

_____. *The Persistent Tradition in New South Politics*. Baton Rouge: Louisiana State University Press, 1975.

Tourgée, Albion W. "The South as a Field for Fiction." *Forum* 6 (December 1888): 404–13.

Twelve Southerners. *I'll Take My Stand: The South and the Agrarian Tradition*. 1930. Introduction by Louis D. Rubin, Jr. Reprint. New York: Harper and Row, 1962.

Wade, John Donald. *Selected Essays and Other Writings*. Edited by Donald Davidson. Athens: University of Georgia Press, 1966.

Weaver, Richard M. *The Southern Tradition at Bay: A History of Post-bellum Thought*. Edited by George Core and M. E. Bradford. New Rochelle, N.Y.: Arlington House, 1968.

Wilson, Edmund. *Patriotic Gore: Studies in the Literature of the American Civil War*. 1962. Reprint. New York: Oxford University Press, 1969.

Woodward, C. Vann. *Origins of the New South, 1877–1913. A History of the South*, edited by Wendell Holmes Stephenson and E. Merton Coulter, vol. 9. 1951. Reprint. Baton Rouge: Louisiana State University Press, 1967.

_____. *Reunion and Reaction: The Compromise of 1877 and the End of Reconstruction*. 1951. Reprint. Boston: Little, Brown and Company, 1966.

_____. *The South in Search of a Philosophy*. Gainesville: University of Florida, 1938.

II. INDIVIDUAL AUTHORS

GEORGE WASHINGTON CABLE

Primary Sources

Dr. Sevier. 1883. Reprint. New York: Charles Scribner's Sons, 1887.

The Grandissimes: A Story of Creole Life. 1880. Reprint. New York: Charles Scribner's Sons, 1895.

John March, Southerner. 1894 [i.e., 1895]. Reprint. New York: Charles Scribner's Sons, 1899.

The Negro Question: A Selection of Writings on Civil Rights in the South. Edited by Arlin Turner. Garden City, N.Y.: Doubleday and Company, 1958.

"The Silent South," Together with "The Freedman's Case in Equity" and "The Convict Lease System." 1885. Reprint. New York: Charles Scribner's Sons, 1907.

Secondary Sources

Butcher, Philip. *George W. Cable: The Northampton Years*. New York: Columbia University Press, 1959.

Rubin, Louis D., Jr. *George W. Cable: The Life and Times of a Southern Heretic*. New York: Pegasus, 1969.

_____. "Politics and the Novel: George W. Cable and the Genteel Tradition." *William Elliott Shoots a Bear: Essays on the Southern*

Literary Imagination. Baton Rouge: Louisiana State University Press, 1975.

————. "The Road to Yoknapatawpha: George W. Cable and *John March, Southerner.*" *Writers of the Modern South: The Faraway Country*. 1963. Reprint. Seattle: University of Washington Press, 1966.

Turner, Arlin. *George W. Cable: A Biography*. Durham: Duke University Press, 1956.

CHARLES WADDELL CHESNUTT

Primary Sources

"Aunt Mimy's Son." *Youth's Companion*, 1 March 1900, pp. 104–105.

The Colonel's Dream. 1905. Reprint. New York: Negro Universities Press, 1970.

The Conjure Woman. New introduction by Robert Farnsworth. 1899. Reprint. Ann Arbor: University of Michigan Press, 1969.

"Dave's Neckliss." In *Southern Writing, 1585–1920*, edited by Richard Beale Davis, C. Hugh Holman, and Louis D. Rubin, Jr. New York: Odyssey Press, 1970.

"The Disfranchisement of the Negro." In *The Negro Problem: A Series of Articles by Representative American Negroes of To-Day*. 1903. Reprint. Miami: Mnemosyne Publishing Company, 1969.

The House behind the Cedars. Introduction by Darwin Turner. 1900. Reprint. New York: Collier Books, 1969.

"McDugald's Mule." *Family Fiction*, 15 January 1887.

"The March of Progress." *Century Magazine* 61 (January, 1901): 422–28.

The Marrow of Tradition. Introduction by Robert Farnsworth. 1901. Reprint. Ann Arbor: University of Michigan Press, 1969.

"Post-Bellum—Pre-Harlem." In *Breaking into Print*, edited by Elmer Adler. New York: Simon and Schuster, 1937.

"A Roman Antique." *Puck*, 17 July 1889, p. 351.

"Tobe's Tribulations." *Southern Workman* 29 (November 1900): 656–64.

"Uncle Peter's House." Cleveland *News and Herald*, December 1885.

"A Victim of Heredity; or, Why the Darkey Loves Chicken." *Self-Culture Magazine* 11 (July 1900): 404–409.

"The Wife of His Youth" and Other Stories of the Color Line. Introduction by Earl Schenck Miers. 1899. Reprint. Ann Arbor: University of Michigan Press, 1968.

Secondary Sources

Andrews, William L. "The Fiction of Charles W. Chesnutt." Ph.D. dissertation, University of North Carolina, 1973.

Britt, David D. "Chesnutt's Conjure Tales: What You See Is What You Get." *College Language Association Journal* 15 (March 1972): 269–83.

Chesnutt, Helen M. *Charles Waddell Chesnutt: Pioneer of the Color Line*. Chapel Hill: University of North Carolina Press, 1952.

Heermance, J. Noel. *Charles W. Chesnutt: America's First Great Black Novelist*. Hamden, Conn.: Archon Books, 1974.

Mason, Julian D., Jr. "Charles W. Chesnutt as Southern Author." *Mississippi Quarterly* 20 (Spring 1967): 77–89.

Meier, August. *Negro Thought in America, 1880–1915: Racial Ideologies in the Age of Booker T. Washington*. 1963. Reprint. Ann Arbor: University of Michigan Press, 1968.

Render, Sylvia Lyons. "Eagle with Clipped Wings: Form and Feeling in the Fiction of Charles Waddell Chesnutt." Ph.D. dissertation, George Peabody College for Teachers, 1962.

JOHN ESTEN COOKE

Primary Source

The Heir of Gaymount: A Novel. New York: Van Evrie, Horton and Company, 1870.

Secondary Sources

Beaty, John O. *John Esten Cooke, Virginian*. New York: Columbia University Press, 1922.

Bratton, Mary Jo Jackson. "John Esten Cooke: The Young Writer and the Old South, 1830–1861." Ph.D. dissertation, University of North Carolina, 1969.

Link, Samuel Albert. *Pioneers of Southern Literature: John Pendleton Kennedy, John Esten Cooke, and Other Southern Novelists*. Nashville: Barbee and Smith, 1898.

Walker, William Edward. "John Esten Cooke: A Critical Biography," Ph.D. dissertation, Vanderbilt University, 1957.

THOMAS DIXON, JR.

Primary Sources

The Clansman: An Historical Romance of the Ku Klux Klan. 1905. Introduction by Thomas D. Clark. Reprint. Lexington: University Press of Kentucky, 1970.
The Leopard's Spots: A Romance of the White Man's Burden, 1865–1900. 1902. Reprint. New York: Grosset and Dunlap, n.d.
The Traitor: A Story of the Fall of the Invisible Empire. New York: Doubleday, Page and Company, 1907.

Secondary Sources

Cook, Raymond Allen. *Fire from the Flint: The Amazing Careers of Thomas Dixon*. Winston-Salem, N.C.: John F. Blair, 1968.
Davenport, F. Garvin, Jr. *The Myth of Southern History: Historical Consciousness in Twentieth-Century Southern Literature*. Nashville: Vanderbilt University Press, 1970.
Harrison, William David. "The Thoughts of Thomas Dixon on Black and White Race Relations in American Society." M.A. thesis, University of South Carolina, 1970.
Wright, J. Zeb. "Thomas Dixon: The Mind of a Southern Apologist." Ph.D. dissertation, George Peabody College for Teachers, 1966.

ELLEN GLASGOW

Primary Sources

The Ancient Law. New York: Doubleday, Page and Company, 1908.
A Certain Measure: An Interpretation of Prose Fiction. New York: Harcourt, Brace and Company, 1943.
The Deliverance: A Romance of the Virginia Tobacco Fields. New York: Doubleday, Page and Company, 1904.
Letters of Ellen Glasgow. Edited by Blair Rouse. New York: Harcourt, Brace and Company, 1958.
The Miller of Old Church. Garden City, N.Y.: Doubleday, Page and Company, 1911.
The Romance of a Plain Man. New York: Macmillan, 1909.
Virginia. Garden City, N.Y.: Doubleday, Page and Company, 1913.
The Voice of the People. 1900. Edited by W. L. Godshalk. Reprint. New Haven: College and University Press, 1972.

The Woman Within. New York: Harcourt, Brace and Company, 1954.

Secondary Sources

Auchincloss, Louis. *Ellen Glasgow*. Minneapolis: University of Minnesota Press, 1964.

Dillard, Richard H. W. "Pragmatic Realism: A Biography of Ellen Glasgow's Novels." Ph.D. dissertation, University of Virginia, 1965.

Godbold, E. Stanly, Jr. *Ellen Glasgow and the Woman Within*. Baton Rouge: Louisiana State University Press, 1972.

McDowell, Frederick P. W. *Ellen Glasgow and the Ironic Art of Fiction*. 1960. Reprint. Madison: University of Wisconsin Press, 1963.

————. "The Prewar Novels." In *Ellen Glasgow: Centennial Essays*, edited by M. Thomas Inge. Charlottesville: University Press of Virginia, 1976.

Moger, Allen W. *Virginia: Bourbonism to Byrd, 1870–1925*. Charlottesville: University Press of Virginia, 1968.

Patterson, Daniel Watkins. "Ellen Glasgow's Use of Virginia History." Ph.D. dissertation, University of North Carolina, 1959.

Raper, J. R. *Without Shelter: The Early Career of Ellen Glasgow*. Baton Rouge: Louisiana State University Press, 1971.

Richards, Marion K. *Ellen Glasgow's Development as a Novelist*. The Hague: Mouton, 1971.

Rouse, Blair. *Ellen Glasgow*. New York: Twayne Publishers, 1962.

Rubin, Louis D., Jr. "Two in Richmond: Ellen Glasgow and James Branch Cabell." In *South: Modern Southern Literature in Its Cultural Setting*, edited by Louis D. Rubin, Jr., and Robert D. Jacobs. Garden City, N.Y.: Doubleday and Company, 1961.

Santas, Joan Foster. *Ellen Glasgow's American Dream*. Charlottesville: University Press of Virginia, 1965.

WILLIAM NATHANIEL HARBEN

Primary Sources

Abner Daniel. New York: Harper and Brothers, 1902.

"American Backgrounds for Fiction: Georgia." *Bookman* 38 (October 1913): 186–92.

Ann Boyd. New York: Harper and Brothers, 1906.

Dixie Hart. 1910. Reprint. New York: A. L. Burt Company, n.d.

The Georgians. New York: Harper and Brothers, 1904.

Gilbert Neal. New York: Harper and Brothers, 1908.

Northern Georgia Sketches. Chicago: A. C. McClurg and Company, 1900.

Pole Baker. New York: Harper and Brothers, 1905.

Secondary Sources

Bush, Robert. "Will N. Harben's Northern Georgia Fiction." *Mississippi Quarterly* 20 (Spring 1967): 103–17.

Harris, Isabella D. "The Southern Mountaineer in American Fiction, 1824–1910." Ph.D. dissertation, Duke University, 1948.

Howells, William Dean. "Mr. Harben's Georgia Fiction." *North American Review* 191 (March 1910): 356–63.

Mercer, Julia. "North Georgia Life in the Fiction of Will N. Harben." M.A. thesis, Duke University, 1938.

Roemer, Kenneth M. "1984 in 1894: Harben's *Land of the Changing Sun.*" *Mississippi Quarterly* 26 (Winter 1972–73): 29–42.

Wade, John Donald. "William Nathaniel Harben." In *Dictionary of American Biography,* edited by Allen Johnson and Dumas Malone, vol. 4. New York: Charles Scribner's Sons, 1959.

JOEL CHANDLER HARRIS

Primary Sources

Balaam and His Master and Other Sketches and Stories. 1891. Reprint. Freeport, N.Y.: Books for Libraries Press, 1969.

The Bishop and the Boogerman. New York: Doubleday, Page and Company, 1909.

The Chronicles of Aunt Minervy Ann. New York: Charles Scribner's Sons, 1899.

The Complete Tales of Uncle Remus. Compiled by Richard Chase. Boston: Houghton Mifflin Company, 1955.

Free Joe and Other Georgian Sketches. 1887. Reprint. New York: P. F. Collier and Son, n.d.

Gabriel Tolliver: A Story of Reconstruction. New York: McClure, Phillips and Company, 1902.

Joel Chandler Harris, Editor and Essayist: Miscellaneous Literary, Political, and Social Writings. Edited by Julia Collier Harris. Chapel Hill: University of North Carolina Press, 1931.

"Letters of Uncle Remus." Edited by Jay B. Hubbell. *Southwestern Review* 23 (January 1938): 216–23.

The Making of a Statesman and Other Stories. New York: McClure, Phillips and Company, 1902.

Mingo and Other Sketches in Black and White. 1884. Reprint. Freeport, N.Y.: Books for Libraries Press, 1971.
"Mr. Sanders to a Boston Capitalist." *World's Work* 1 (December 1900): 196–99.
"Progress—in the Best and Highest Sense." *Uncle Remus's–The Home Magazine* 24 (January 1909): 7–8.
Tales of the Home Folks in Peace and War. Boston: Houghton Mifflin Company, 1898.
Told by Uncle Remus: New Stories of the Old Plantation. 1905. Reprint. New York: Grosset and Dunlap, n.d.
Uncle Remus: His Songs and His Sayings. 1880. Reprint. New York: Grosset and Dunlap, 1921.

Secondary Sources

Cousins, Paul M. *Joel Chandler Harris: A Biography*. Baton Rouge: Louisiana State University Press, 1968.
Harris, Julia Collier. *The Life and Letters of Joel Chandler Harris*. Boston: Houghton Mifflin Company, 1918.
Herndon, Jerry Allen. "Social Comment in the Writings of Joel Chandler Harris." Ph.D. dissertation, Duke University, 1966.
Rubin, Louis D., Jr. "Uncle Remus and the Ubiquitous Rabbit." *William Elliott Shoots a Bear: Essays on the Southern Literary Imagination*. Baton Rouge: Louisiana State University Press, 1975.
Smith, Herbert F. "Joel Chandler Harris's Contributions to *Scribner's Monthly* and *Century Magazine*, 1880–1887." *Georgia Historical Quarterly* 47 (June 1963): 169–79.
Wade, John Donald. "Profits and Losses in the Life of Joel Chandler Harris." *Selected Essays and Other Writings*. Edited by Donald Davidson. Athens: University of Georgia Press, 1966.

PAUL HAMILTON HAYNE

Primary Sources

A Collection of Hayne Letters. Edited by Daniel Morley McKeithan. Austin: University of Texas Press, 1944.
The Correspondence of Bayard Taylor and Paul Hamilton Hayne. Edited by Charles Duffy. Baton Rouge: Louisiana State University Press, 1945.
"Last Poems." Durham. Duke University. Hayne Papers.
"Lyric: Requested by the Southern Exposition at Louisville." *Home and Farm: A Semi-Monthly Record for Farmers* 8 (1 October 1883): 1.

Poems. Complete edition. Boston: D. Lothrop and Company, 1882.
"Seven Unpublished Letters of Paul Hamilton Hayne." Edited by
  William Stanley Hoole. *Georgia Historical Quarterly* 22 (September
  1938): 273–85.
"A Southern Genteelist: Letters of Paul Hamilton Hayne to Julia C.
  R. Dorr." Edited by Charles Duffy. *South Carolina Historical and
  Genealogical Magazine* 52 (April 1951): 65–73, (July 1951): 154–65,
  (October 1951): 207–17; 53 (January 1952): 19–30.

Secondary Sources

Anderson, Charles Roberts. "Charles Gayarré and Paul Hamilton
  Hayne: The Last Literary Cavaliers." In *American Studies in Honor
  of William Kenneth Boyd*. Edited by David Kelly Jackson. Durham:
  Duke University Press, 1940.
Carter, John Archer. "Paul Hayne's Sonnet 'To the New South.'"
  Georgia Historical Quarterly 48 (June 1964): 193–95.
Flory, Claude R. "Paul Hamilton Hayne and the New South."
  Georgia Historical Quarterly 46 (December 1962): 388–94.
Green, Claud B. "Charles Colcock Jones, Jr., and Paul Hamilton
  Hayne." In *Georgians in Profile: Historical Essays in Honor of Ellis
  Merton Coulter*. Edited by Horace Montgomery. Athens: Univer-
  sity of Georgia Press, 1958.
Hardendorff, Victor Hall. "Paul Hamilton Hayne and the North."
  M.A. thesis, Duke University, 1942.
Moore, Rayburn S. *Paul Hamilton Hayne*. New York: Twayne Pub-
  lishers, 1972.

SIDNEY LANIER

Primary Sources

The Centennial Edition of the Works of Sidney Lanier. Vol. 1, *Poems and
  Poem Outlines*, edited by Charles R. Anderson. Vol. 5, *Tiger-Lilies
  and Southern Prose*, edited by Garland Greever. Vols. 7–10, *Letters*, edited by Charles R. Anderson and Aubrey H. Starke. Baltimore: Johns Hopkins University Press, 1945.

Secondary Sources

De Bellis, Jack A. *Sidney Lanier*. New York: Twayne Publishers,
  1972.
Mims, Edwin. *Sidney Lanier*. Boston: Houghton Mifflin Company,
  1905.

Ransom, John Crowe. "Hearts and Heads." *American Review* 2 (March 1934): 554–71.

Rubin, Louis D., Jr. "The Passion of Sidney Lanier." *William Elliott Shoots a Bear: Essays on the Southern Literary Imagination*. Baton Rouge: Louisiana State University Press, 1975.

Starke, Aubrey Harrison. "The Agrarians Deny a Leader." *American Review* 2 (March 1934): 534–53.

————. *Sidney Lanier: A Biographical and Critical Study*. Chapel Hill: University of North Carolina Press, 1933.

Tate, Allen. "A Southern Romantic." *New Republic* 76 (30 August 1933): 67–70.

Warren, Robert Penn. "The Blind Poet: Sidney Lanier." *American Review* 2 (November 1933): 27–45.

THOMAS NELSON PAGE

Primary Sources

Gordon Keith. 1903. Reprint. New York: Charles Scribner's Sons, 1905.

In Ole Virginia; or, Marse Chan and Other Stories. New York: Charles Scribner's Sons, 1887.

John Fox and Tom Page as They Were: Letters, an Address, and an Essay. Edited by Harriet R. Holman. Miami: Field Research Projects, n.d.

The Negro: The Southerner's Problem. New York: Charles Scribner's Sons, 1904.

The Old Dominion: Her Making and Her Manners. New York: Charles Scribner's Sons, 1908.

The Old South: Essays Social and Political. 1892. Reprint. New York: Charles Scribner's Sons, 1900.

Red Rock: A Chronicle of Reconstruction. 1898. Reprint. New York: Grosset and Dunlap, n.d.

Secondary Sources

Griffith, Benjamin W. "Csardas at Salt Springs: Southern Culture in 1888." *Georgia Review* 26 (Spring 1972): 53–59.

Gross, Theodore L. *Thomas Nelson Page*. New York: Twayne Publishers, 1967.

Holman, Harriet R. "The Literary Career of Thomas Nelson Page, 1884–1910." Ph.D. dissertation, Duke University, 1947.

King, James Kimball. "George Washington Cable and Thomas Nelson Page: Two Literary Approaches to the New South." Ph.D. dissertation, University of Wisconsin, 1964.

Pond, Major J. B. *Eccentricities of Genius: Memories of Famous Men and Women of the Platform and Stage.* New York: G. W. Dillingham Company, 1900.

Sowder, William J. "Gerald W. Johnson, Thomas Nelson Page, and the South." *Mississippi Quarterly* 14 (Fall 1961): 197–203.

FRANCIS HOPKINSON SMITH

Primary Source

Colonel Carter of Cartersville. 1891. Reprint. Boston: Houghton Mifflin Company, 1900.

Secondary Sources

Page, Thomas Nelson. "Francis Hopkinson Smith." *Scribner's Magazine* 58 (September 1915): 305–13.

Patton, John S. "Francis Hopkinson Smith." In *Library of Southern Literature.* Edited by Edwin Anderson Alderman and Joel Chandler Harris. Vol. 11. New Orleans: Martin and Hoyt Company, 1907.

Quinn, Arthur Hobson. *American Fiction: An Historical and Critical Survey.* New York: Appleton-Century-Crofts, 1936.

White, Courtland Y., III. "Francis Hopkinson Smith." In *Dictionary of American Biography.* Edited by Dumas Malone. Vol. 9. New York: Charles Scribner's Sons, 1935.

MARK TWAIN [SAMUEL LANGHORNE CLEMENS]

Primary Sources

A Connecticut Yankee at King Arthur's Court. 1889. Introduction by Justin Kaplan. Reprint. Baltimore: Penguin Books, 1971.

The Gilded Age: A Tale of Today. With Charles Dudley Warner. 1873. Introduction by Justin Kaplan. Reprint. Seattle: University of Washington Press, 1968.

Life on the Mississippi. 1883. Reprint. New York: Harper and Row, 1917.

Secondary Sources

French, Bryant Morey. *Mark Twain and "The Gilded Age": The Book That Named an Era*. Dallas: Southern Methodist University Press, 1965.

Howells, William Dean. *My Mark Twain: Reminiscences and Criticisms*. Edited by Marilyn Austin Baldwin. 1910. Reprint. Baton Rouge: Louisiana State University Press, 1967.

Kaplan, Justin. *Mr. Clemens and Mark Twain*. New York: Simon and Schuster, 1966.

————, ed. *Mark Twain: A Profile*. New York: Hill and Wang, 1967.

Morgan, H. Wayne. *American Writers in Rebellion: From Mark Twain to Dreiser*. New York: Hill and Wang, 1965.

Neider, Charles, ed. *The Adventures of Colonel Sellers*. Garden City, N.Y.: Doubleday and Company, 1965.

Pettit, Arthur G. "Mark Twain and the Negro, 1867–1869." *Journal of Negro History* 56 (April 1971): 88–96.

————. *Mark Twain and the South*. Lexington: University Press of Kentucky, 1974.

————. "Mark Twain, Unreconstructed Southerner, and His View of the Negro, 1835–1860." *Rocky Mountain Social Science Journal* 7 (April 1970): 17–28.

————. "Mark Twain's Attitude toward the Negro in the West, 1861–1867." *Western Historical Quarterly* 1 (January 1970): 51–62.

Smith, Henry Nash. *Mark Twain: The Development of a Writer*. Cambridge: Harvard University Press, Belknap Press, 1962.

————. *Mark Twain's Fable of Progress: Political and Economic Ideas in "A Connecticut Yankee."* New Brunswick, N.J.: Rutgers University Press, 1964.

Turner, Arlin. "James Lampton, Mark Twain's Model for Colonel Sellers." *Modern Language Notes* 70 (December 1955): 592–94.

————. "Mark Twain and the South: An Affair of Love and Anger." *Southern Review* 4 (April 1968): 493–519.

Warren, Robert Penn. "Mark Twain." *Southern Review* 8 (July 1972): 459–92.

Wecter, Dixon. *Sam Clemens of Hannibal*. Boston: Houghton Mifflin Company, 1952.

INDEX